The Terrorists

Also by Milton Meltzer

The Human Rights Book
The Truth About the Ku Klux Klan
The Jewish Americans: A History in Their Own Words,
   1650–1950
The Hispanic Americans
The Chinese Americans
All Times, All Peoples: A World History of Slavery
Never to Forget: The Jews of the Holocaust
In Their Own Words: A History of the American Negro
   Volume I: 1619–1865
   Volume II: 1865–1916
   Volume III: 1916–1966
Langston Hughes: A Biography
A Pictorial History of Black Americans
   (with Langston Hughes and C. Eric Lincoln)

DEATH TOLL AT 16
IN ULSTER BOMBING

ROME BOMB ROCKS
LEBANESE EMBASSY

Bonn Is Fearful
Of Bulgaria Tie
With Terrorists

Pro-Israeli West Bank Official Wounded by B

U.S. Military Housing Area in Germany Is Bombed

3 Italians Accused
Of Red Brigades Work

Toll in India Bombing
Now Reported at 19

F.A.L.N. Puerto Rican Terrorists
Suspected in New Year Bombings

4 With Arab Passpc
Held in London A

War of Terror
By Albanians
In Yugoslavia

Turkey Says It Will Stop
Terrorism by Armenians

3 Bombs Hit Buenos Aires

ast 6

Terrorists Kill a Top General in Madrid

2 Members of Red Brigades
Are Captured by Italian Police

Toronto Group Says
It Set Off Factory Blast

HAITI BOMB BLAST
KILLS 10 IN CAPITAL

9 Turks Seize Cologne Consulate;
Surrender After a 16-Hour Siege

British Soldier Killed by Bomb
Hidden in a Barrier in Belfast

Beirut Bomb Kills 12 at French Embassy

Bombs in Z
and

OMB KILLS
POLICEMEN

The Count: 25 Dead, 373 Wounded
By Terrorists In Last Two Years

Brink's Inquiry Said to Reveal a Web of Radical Cr

West German Police Seize Most-Wanted Terrorist

Four Bombs Explode in Manhattan
And Brooklyn, Injuring 3 Officers

Bombs Rock I.B.M

Milton Meltzer The Terrorists

HARPER & ROW, PUBLISHERS

The Terrorists
Copyright © 1983 by Milton Meltzer
All rights reserved. No part of this book may be used or reproduced in any manner whatsoever without written permission except in the case of brief quotations embodied in critical articles and reviews. Printed in the United States of America. For information address Harper & Row, Publishers, Inc., 10 East 53rd Street, New York, N.Y. 10022. Published simultaneously in Canada by Fitzhenry & Whiteside Limited, Toronto.

Library of Congress Cataloging in Publication Data
Meltzer, Milton, date
    The terrorists.

    Summary: A historical survey of terrorism, investigating the tactics of modern terror organizations and totalitarian regimes and evaluating the morality and political effectiveness of their violent actions.
    1. Terrorism—History—Juvenile literature.
    2. Terrorism—Juvenile literature.   [1. Terrorism.
    2. History, Modern—20th century]   I. Title.
HV6431.M44 1983   303.6′25′09   82-48858
ISBN 0-06-024193-4
ISBN 0-06-024194-2 (lib. bdg.)

Designed by Al Cetta
1   2   3   4   5   6   7   8   9   10
First Edition

CONTENTS

Police search beneath a Brink's armored truck for clues to the 1981 armed robbery of the $1.6 million it carried. In the background is the covered body of a Brink's guard, killed by the holdup gang who called themselves "freedom fighters."

Chapter 1

Anyone Is Fair Game

That Tuesday night—it was October 20, 1981—sitting comfortably at home in Manhattan, I switched on the TV to catch up with the day's happenings.

The leadoff news item was a sensational robbery and triple murder.

A gang of men and women had ambushed a Brink's armored car outside a bank in nearby Nyack, stolen $1.6 million from it, and killed a Brink's guard. Ten minutes later, as they made their getaway in a U-Haul truck, some of the thieves were stopped at a police roadblock. Several gunmen with automatic weapons leaped from the rear of the U-Haul, spraying bullets, and two of the policemen at the roadblock fell dead. Almost the instant the firing started, a woman jumped unarmed from the cab of the U-Haul and began running off. She was caught by a New York corrections officer who happened to be driving by when he heard the gunshots and stopped.

Within an hour of the shootings three of the other thieves, fleeing in a speeding car, smashed into a concrete retaining wall. The police who arrested them found bulletproof vests, ski masks, and canvas bank money bags in the car.

This is yet another of those holdups and killings that pepper the news all too often, I thought.

The next morning it had turned into something quite different. The suspects picked up on the scene, and the others arrested soon after, were not your everyday bank robbers. These people included former members of the Black Panthers, organized in 1966 by black youth in militant protest against racism, and two women and a man (Kathy Boudin, Judith Clark, and David Gilbert) identified as members of a radical group that had been active in the late 1960s and early '70s. The Weather Underground, they were called back then. Those were the years of the furious protests against the Vietnam War. The Weather people had taken part in street demonstrations, assaults on police, symbolic bombings of public buildings. But by the late 1970s, with the war ended, their radical membership, never large, had dwindled to a handful and then disappeared.

Yet here they were again on the front pages and the TV screen, and this time with guns blazing and victims dying in the street. Another "Bonnie and Clyde" gang? No—"we are revolutionaries, freedom fighters," they said in court. As the legal proceedings began, their sympathizers marched around the courthouse carrying banners. One of the demonstrators told reporters that the Brink's holdup and shootout was "a revolutionary expropriation, like George Washington's and Patrick Henry's, to finance their revolution. Our revolution is to get back a small portion of what was taken from us."

Like almost everyone else the day the story broke, I was horrified by the robbery and murders. What had brought supposedly intelligent people to do these things? Could political activists believe theft and killing were all part of the game? What kind of revolution did this symbolize? What did these people want? What did they hope for? What kind of world, I wondered, would they make if they ever got power?

I realized that what had happened in the Brink's case was not new. Political extremists—of both the right and the left—had financed their plans by robbery, and not hesitated to kill, before this time. But how common is political terrorism? How far back does it go? Is it a worldwide phenomenon?

Terrorism is as old as humankind. It began thousands of years ago, and it goes on up to this minute. On the single day of April 2, 1982, *The New York Times* carried six brief stories about terrorism around the globe:

> In Northern Ireland two British soldiers were slain in ambush by the IRA.
>
> In Lebanon a terrorist band claimed credit for a

machine-gun attack on the Israeli Embassy in Paris a few days before.

In Argentina three bombs smashed a Buenos Aires hotel, a bank, and a store.

In Greece a bomb exploded outside the Athens home of the U.S. Ambassador.

In Turkey the military arrested 29 people for trying to revive a leftist terrorist gang.

In West Germany a woman student was arrested for giving support to the terrorist group that attacked the U.S. Army's European commanding general.

All in one day . . .

Using the *The New York Times* as source, a scholar has estimated that some 10,000 people were killed by terrorist actions in the decade 1968–78. Going back through history we will find that champions of many causes have chosen to use political terror.

Before going on, however, let's pause at that adjective, "political." Politics refers to the ways in which people of any state or group try to determine or control its public policy. "People" means us, ourselves. We're all involved in politics in one way or another. We take this or that course of action to advance or protect our interests. As members of student organizations or governments, we campaign for the candidates or policies we prefer. As individual citizens we act through parties or pressure groups to influence the election or appointment of those who manage the affairs of state—legis-lators, judges, mayors, governors, presidents, many others. Once they are in office, we try to influence their official acts and statements. If we're passive, if we don't move, our interests are affected by the actions of others. The question really is not *whether* to take part in politics, but rather *how*? And for what goals?

There can be a variety of political ways to act to achieve a goal. Which way we choose often depends on the climate of the times and on our own motives, our own personalities.

The basic means of political struggle haven't changed much over the centuries. Only the technology has. At one end the means include voting and attempts to influence opinion by spreading information and ideas. This can be done by word of mouth, by printed material, by speeches, demonstrations, marches, rallies, lobbying, radio, TV, films. And the style can vary from offering the simple facts to rabble-rousing, lies, and slander. At the other end the methods chosen can include conspiracies, assassinations, uprisings, guerrilla warfare, revolution.

Politics is as old as the unending conflict between the "ins" and the "outs." Those in power strive to maintain their place; those out of power try to take their place. The struggle can be conducted peacefully or violently. Acts of violence kill or injure persons or do significant damage to property. In time of war, of course, states use violence against one another. And in peacetime they use authorized violence to execute convicted criminals. But violence in the discussion of terrorism means "the illegitimate use of coercion, resulting, or intended to result in, the death, injury, restraint, or intimidation of persons or the destruction or seizure of property." Illegal violence can be used by groups or by individuals, and by the state itself when it ignores its own constitution or laws. The stress is on the unauthorized and illegal aspect.

The dictionary defines terror as "the state of extreme fear; fear that agitates the body and mind; violent dread; fright." Terrorism is the exploitation of a state of intense fear, caused by the systematic use of violent means by a party or group, to get into power or to maintain power. The party or group inspires the state of fear through acts—bombings, kidnappings, hijackings, assassinations—that terrorize. Terrorism is a policy of intimidation. It often results from frustration, failure to reach goals by normal, peaceful means.

These terms—terrorism, terrorist, terrorize—didn't come into common use until after the French applied them to their revolutionary period of 1793–98. In that time the words came to define those revolutionaries who used terror to impose their views or to govern. Then, as before and since, the violence was directed against the group holding power, or against other rivals for power.

It may seem that there is no difference between terrorists and an armed insurrection. But there is. The armed uprising of part of a people seeks to confront the armed force of the government. The terrorists do not want that; they know they are too few and too weak to survive such open combat. Their aim is to use terror to weaken the will of the community or government and to undermine morale. It is a form of secret and undeclared warfare—psychological warfare, really.

The violence of terrorists is often used indiscriminately. All men, women, and children (as we shall see), regardless of their place or function in society, may be looked upon as potential victims. And the victims are unable to do anything to avoid their injury or destruction, because the terrorist has his own code of values by which he judges whom to hurt. The conventions of war—the rights of neutrals, noncombatants, hostages, prisoners of war—have no standing in the eyes of the terrorist. Anyone is fair game.

It should be clear simply from casual reading of the press that terrorism is not the monopoly of any ideology or cause. Terror has become the weapon of many different ideologies (from extreme right to extreme left), religions, ethnic groups, nationalists. In the twentieth century Mussolini, Stalin, and Hitler pioneered many techniques and tactics of terrorism as an auxiliary weapon for grabbing and hanging on to power.

But let's go back much earlier in time to see the beginnings of terrorism.

Chapter 2

Murder for Progress

Brutal tyrants were among the earliest targets of political terrorism. They were rulers who exercised absolute power over their subjects in an arbitrary way. By excessive taxation, by injustice, by cruel punishment, they placed such burdens on their people that they often brought about what is called "tyrannicide"—the murder of the tyrant. The killers of such kings saw it as their political duty to remove the evil of a tyrant ruler.

For thousands of years assassins have killed public figures for such political reasons. The Assyrian king Sennacherib was murdered by his two sons. The tyrant of Athens, Hipparchus, was slain by two patriots. Caesar was stabbed to death by Brutus for seizing dictatorial powers. In ancient Palestine shortly after the time of Christ, the Sicarii terrorists—Jewish nationalists who were violently anti-Roman—assassinated the moderate members of the Jewish Peace Party.

That very word, "assassin," has its roots in the first organized group to use murder systematically for a cause it believed to be righteous. This was the Assassins, the famous Muslim sect who appeared in Persia and Syria in the eleventh century. It is from their name that the modern word assassin comes. The word derives from the Syrian word *hashishi*. (That was the drug hashish, to which the Assassins may have been addicted.) They were part of the Islamic sect of the Shia, which warred against the other major sect, the Sunni. The Assassins believed they had a religious duty to kill the unrighteous. Each act of murder was a sacred obligation. Their weapon was always the dagger. It required killing at close quarters, which made capture quite likely. But such suicidal acts meant they would not only help overthrow a corrupt order, but guarantee their own salvation in the afterlife.

How the Assassins operated has set the model for terrorist groups ever since. Their organization was highly disciplined. They lived by a strict code of secrecy. They stressed popular propaganda, spreading their beliefs to the people. They used terror to force local political authorities into compromise or cooperation. Their targets for murder were key people of the Sunni order, both its religious and political leaders. They failed to destroy the Sunni orthodoxy, but their tactics survived to be imitated by other terrorists all over the world.

The rulers of Europe did not need the example of

the Middle East to encourage them to resort to political murder. By the Middle Ages acts of tyrannicide were justified to save Christian society from the rule of evil men. During the Renaissance it became common to justify the murder of political and religious enemies by accusing them of defying the laws of God.

It was during the French Revolution of 1789 that terrorism was made into the modern political weapon we know today. Philosophers of the eighteenth century had developed ideas about the people's right to liberty and justice. As Jefferson put it in the Declaration of Independence, "We hold these Truths to be self-evident, that all Men are created equal, that they are endowed by their Creator with certain unalienable Rights, that among these are Life, Liberty, and the Pursuit of Happiness." When any government violates those aims, the people have a right to revolt against it, said this new philosophy. In the early period of the French Revolution mobs had taken vengence against the aristocracy by spontaneous acts of violence. But with the struggle for power among the various leaders of the revolution, organized terror came into use. Men who failed to achieve their political goals through peaceful means substituted terror.

It was the Jacobin party that introduced the idea of a *policy* of terror to smash the opposition to their policy. In the Reign of Terror (1793–94) an army of informers was recruited to round up anyone on the faintest suspicion of treachery. The Terror was carried from Paris into the provinces, and great numbers of suspects were

The elegant young lawyer Maximilien Robespierre, a leader of the French Revolution who initiated the Reign of Terror. He used the guillotine to dispose of opponents and was himself executed under its blade.

butchered without trial. In one district victims were chained together and shot at by cannon. The wounded were finished off by bullet. The dead were buried in mass graves of quicklime. Even mass drownings in the rivers took place.

Historians estimate that 40,000 were killed by the guillotine and other means, and 400,000 men, women, and children were imprisoned in dungeons. (Large as these numbers are, they pale next to the huge loss of citizens' lives caused by the policies of Stalin, Hitler, Mao, and other dictators of the twentieth century.)

What was new about the French terrorism was its use as a method of *preventive* repression. Not simply individuals came under suspicion, but whole classes, groups, parties were labeled *potential* enemies of the Revolution. Another innovation was terrorization of thought. The people in power tried to control ideas, art, literature, and the press by censorship, by intimidation, by terror.

Such revolutionary "justice" was exercised upon the mere whim or will of the terrorists. This was different from the individual executions of the Muslim Assassins or the tyrannicides. Now terrorists were murdering anyone they chose in the name of the collective good of the people. The politics of the revolutionaries in power decided who would live and who would die. They took unto themselves the right to determine what the people wanted, and to carry that out.

In the name of a "sacred mission" thousands were ruined, tortured, and murdered. A White Terror

Under mere suspicion of disloyalty to the French Revolution, thousands of victims were carted off to execution.

(meaning from the political right wing) took over, which continued the killing, only this time of the Red (left-wing) terrorists. In the end, the original revolutionary leaders themselves fell one after another before the guillotine. What had begun as a movement of liberation turned into butchery by rival terrorisms. The final out-come was a coup that made Napoleon military dictator of France.

One of the figures of the French Revolution became a model for revolutionaries of the nineteenth century. Gracchus Babeuf, the son of a poor peasant, was an archivist. He supported the Revolution but believed that in establishing only political equality, it had not gone far enough. Private property was the root of all evil, he said. Justice and liberty were not possible with-out complete social and economic equality. In Paris he organized a committee of soldiers and workmen around a program of economic equality, a kind of primitive socialism. When his radical group was banned, he de-veloped a secret society to overthrow the government by force. In his plan his committee, acting as the van-guard of the people, would seize power, wipe out all opposition, and then, through propaganda, convince the people that Babeuf expressed their true will. He badly overestimated his popular support, and was be-trayed and executed. New generations of revolution-aries would, like Babeuf, assume they knew what was best for the people and, without consulting them, act in their name.

Babeuf's lieutenant, Philippe Buonarroti, a handsome Italian aristocrat, survived prison and exile to pass on Babeuf's ideas about conspiracy. Secret societies multiplied in the early nineteenth century. Those in Italy especially, called the Carbonari, were notorious for their use of the dagger and poison.

The most important case for terrorism published in that time was Karl Heinzen's article called "Murder." Heinzen, a radical democrat from Germany, wrote just after the European revolutions of 1848. He blamed their failure on the reluctance by radicals to be ruthless. "Murder is the principal agent of historical progress," he said. Yes, he admitted that the killing of another human being was considered to be a crime against humanity. "But," he went on:

Against our enemies with their executions and soldiers . . . we are able to achieve precious little with our humanity and our ideas of justice. . . . Let us take the moral horror out of the great historical tool. . . . Once one has overcome the objection that murder per se is a crime, all that remains is to believe one is in the right against one's enemy and to possess the power to obliterate him. . . . It is no great step from this necessity . . . to condemning hundreds of thousands to the scaffold in the interests of humanity. . . .

Once killing has been accepted, the moral stance is seen to have no foundation, the legal is seen to be ineffectual, and the political alone is of any significance. . . . To have a conscience with regard to the destruction of reactionaries is to be totally unprincipled. They wreak destruction, in any way they can, thereby

obliging us to respond in kind as defenders of justice
and humanity. . . . Even if we have to blow up half a
continent or spill a sea of blood, in order to finish off
the barbarian party, we should have no scruples about
doing it.

Appearing first in 1849, Heinzen's justification for
terror was reprinted and quoted innumerable times by
the advocates of direct action. Heinzen himself took a
more peaceful path, emigrating to America. There he
edited a German-language newspaper and died in Boston in 1880.

Chapter 3

Propaganda by the Deed

Karl Heinzen's ideas took root in the second half of the nineteenth century. Terrorism of several kinds appeared throughout Europe and America. In one sense it sprang from the same source—the rise of democracy and nationalism. Conditions that made people unhappy had existed for centuries. But few had felt there was much chance to do anything about them. As ideas about democracy and freedom and national liberation spread, old grievances became less and less tolerable. Protest movements arose to make demands of the ruling classes and the governing powers. When progress was slow, some of the rebels turned to terrorism.

Among the most important branches of the revolutionary movement were Marxism and anarchism. Both are philosophies that deal with political, social, and economic life. They are complex and contradictory, and this is not the place to go into them in any detail. Their impact upon the use of terrorism is what concerns us here.

The idea of anarchism can be traced back to the ancient Greeks. From them comes the word: *an*, meaning not, and *archos*, meaning government or rule. Hence *anarchia*, no-government, nonrule. Zeno, a philosopher of classical Greece, was the first anarchist thinker; he thought it desirable and possible to have a harmonious society without any kind of rule from above. Such confidence assumed that human beings and their society could be made perfect. For if people are naturally wicked, greedy, violent, then police and armies are necessary to keep the peace. So the true anarchist has to be an idealist.

The anarchists themselves don't agree on what a state of anarchy is, or how such a society would be achieved. Anarchism has never been tried in any nation, so there is no model for either success or failure. What they do agree on is that freedom of the individual is all-important. Whatever restricts human freedom should be done away with. They see the greatest barrier to that freedom as the state itself. No government is good, for it exerts tyrannical rule over the individual. And even in a democracy, where people vote, the majority rules over the minority.

One of anarchism's fiercest advocates in the nineteenth century was Mikhail Bakunin (1814–76). The son of an aristocratic Russian family, he had a happy

Mikhail Bakunin, the Russian anarchist, photographed by Nadar in Paris. The "Russian Bear,"
as he called himself, was "prepared to wade
through seas of blood" to gain his political goals.

country childhood, and grew up to be a great bear of a man, but violently rebellious. Later he said his hatred for every limit on personal liberty could be laid to the fact that his mother was a tyrant. During his twenties in Paris he met the international set of radical intellectuals who were living there, including Karl Marx. He saw no hope for change in his native land except through an armed revolution. He wrote:

> We reject all legislation, all authority, and all privileged, licensed, official and legal influence, even though arising from universal suffrage, convinced that it can turn only to the advantage of a dominant minority of exploiters against the interests of the immense majority in subjection to them.

Bakunin wanted to abolish "the centralizing and domineering state" and demanded "the absolute destruction" of all its institutions. His special appeal for young people—then and now—has been great because of his trumpeting call for the struggle against all authority.

What he was against is clear. What he was for is cloudy. But roughly, he saw the future society as one in which the factories would belong to the people working in them (not to the state, as in today's Communist countries). The workers would organize themselves into local associations, then unite into larger ones. And so too would locally elected councils unite in ever higher ones up to a council for the whole country.

A marvelous mob orator, Bakunin talked revolution

all over Europe. But he was more than a talker, and he promoted revolutionary uprisings wherever he could—in Russia, Germany, France, Italy, Austria. He took part in five revolutions himself. He believed that destroying governments and their harmful institutions was the highest creative act. Revolution was so essential that no personal interest, no religious scruple, no moral conviction, should stand in its way. "The joy of destruction is a creative joy," he wrote. He urged the use of poison, the dagger, the noose, the bullet, the bomb, because "the revolution sanctifies everything that is done in this struggle."

In a leaflet Bakunin wrote in the early 1870s, he preached systematic assassination and what came to be known as "propaganda by the deed." He said:

> We believe only in those who show their devotion to the cause of the revolution by deeds, without fear of torture or imprisonment, because we renounce all words that are not immediately followed by deeds. We have no further use for aimless propaganda that does not set itself a definite time and place for realization of the aims of revolution. What is more, it stands in our way and we shall make every effort to combat it. . . . We shall silence by force the chatterers who refuse to understand this.

It was while living in exile in Geneva that the middle-aged Bakunin acquired a fervent young Russian disciple. Sergei Nechayev (1847–82) was the son of a craftsman and a peasant woman. At nine he went to work in a textile mill. Helped by people impressed by his brilliance, he got to Moscow University, where he pledged himself to destroy tsarism. He was taken with Babeuf's terrorism methods and formed a secret cell of revolutionary students. They were impressed by romantic tales he invented about having been imprisoned for radical activity, and of his success in escaping his jailers. In 1869, when the police were hot on his trail, he fled to Geneva, where he met Bakunin. Taken by Nechayev's ruthless energy, Bakunin swallowed his lies and boasted to his friends of this "magnificent young fanatic."

Nechayev convinced Bakunin that he had escaped from the dreaded Peter and Paul fortress and been sent to him by a revolutionary committee that controlled a Russia-wide network of conspirators. Matching that invention, Bakunin enrolled the young man in the World Revolutionary Alliance, a nonexistent organization, making him Agent No. 2771 of the Russian section. Like children playing games, they became partners in an imaginary alliance and began writing revolutionary pamphlets for circulation in their homeland. One of the pieces, *Principles of Revolution*, preached indiscriminate destruction and justified the use of any means to attain the revolution's goal. "We recognize no other activity but the work of extermination," says *Principles*, "but we admit that the forms in which this activity will show itself will be extremely varied—poison, the knife, the rope, etc."

More extreme was *The Revolutionary Catechism*, written by Nechayev, probably with some help from

Bakunin. It deals with Nechayev's ideas about how to become a model revolutionary: You needed to create a ruthless ego dedicated to revolution by the practice of terrorism.

Here are some of the elements that make up Nechayev's formula for a terrorist revolutionary:

> The revolutionary is a lost man; he has no interests of his own, no feelings, no habits, no belongings. . . . Everything in him is absorbed by a single, exclusive interest, one thought, one passion—the revolution. . . .
>
> He has broken every tie with the civil order, with the educated world and all laws, conventions and generally accepted conditions, and with the ethics of this world. He will be an implacable enemy of this world; and if he continue to live in it, it must be only in order to destroy it. . . .
>
> The revolutionary knows only one science, that of destruction. . . .
>
> For him, everything that allows the triumph of the revolution is moral, and everything that stands in its way is immoral. . . .
>
> With no pity for the state and for the privileged world in general, he must himself expect no pity. Every day he must be prepared for death. He must be prepared to bear torture.
>
> All the tender feelings of family life, of friendship, love, gratitude and even honour must be stilled in him by a single passion for the revolutionary cause . . . day and night he must have one single thought, one single purpose: merciless destruction . . . he must always be prepared to die, and to kill with his own hands. . . .

How to work this transformation? Nechayev's answer: By drawing close to the people who continued fighting tsarism not just in words but by deeds: "We must ally ourselves with the doughty world of brigands who, in Russia, are the only real revolutionaries."

Nechayev soon returned secretly to Russia and formed a revolutionary organization of university students. When one of its members refused to carry out an order Nechayev gave him, Nechayev murdered him. The victim's body was found and all of Nechayev's comrades arrested. Nechayev escaped across the border and wandered about Europe, preaching the use of blackmail, robbery, and murder to wreck the established order. Some said he used those methods himself to take care of his own needs. The Swiss deported him to Russia, where he was tried for murder and sentenced to twenty years in the terrible Peter and Paul fortress, to be followed by exile to Siberia for the rest of his life. He died in prison ten years later, shortly after the assassination of Tsar Alexander II.

More important than Bakunin in the history of the Russian revolutionary movement was the writer Alexander Herzen (1812–70). He too came of an aristocratic family, and like Bakunin devoted his life to rebellion against every form of oppression. Both men placed the idea of individual liberty at the center of their thought and action. Herzen more than anyone else created the tradition of systematic revolutionary agitation. But unlike Bakunin he would not sacrifice the freedom of individuals to the abstract idea of revolution. He attacked

Alexander Herzen, photographed by Nadar while in exile in Paris. A founder of the revolutionary movement in Russia, he believed no utopian goal could justify the suppression of liberty or the use of violence.

Bakunin and the terrorists for their readiness to slaughter people today for the sake of "future happiness." He saw how indifferent his friend Bakunin was to the fate of individual human beings. Bakunin was ready to play with human lives for the sake of social experiment. While such revolutionaries professed horror at tsarism's arbitrary violence and its victimization of innocent persons, they themselves showed a lust for revolution for revolution's sake. They protested against poverty and oppression in the abstract, but the fate of real people, their rights and liberties, did not greatly concern them.

Cynical elitists like Nechayev insisted that the uneducated and ignorant masses must be saved by any available means against their own foolish wishes, even if it meant using deceit, fraud, or violence. The majority of radicals in Nechayev's time did not agree. They were horrified by such tactics. Even the noblest ends would be destroyed by the use of monstrous means.

The Russian revolutionaries wished to train their followers to destroy the tsarist system and cut down all obstacles to equality and democracy. With themselves in power they would explain to the masses what they had done and why. Then the masses, ignorant though they might be now, would understand at least enough to let themselves be organized into the new, free, socialist society.

But, Herzen asked again and again, suppose the masses, after the revolution, fail to see things the same way you do? What then? The terrorist wing of the radicals had no doubts. Terrorism and more terrorism would achieve complete anarchist liberty. That ideal condition would be imposed at first by the power of the new state, after which that state would swiftly dissolve itself.

To which Herzen replied, if the aim of the revolution is to liberate, how can it use the weapons of despots? Wouldn't you only enslave those you hoped to make free? You would be applying a remedy more destructive than the disease! In trying to break the chains of tsarism, you would put in their place the no-less-binding chains of the revolutionary minority. No, Herzen insisted, the only hope for a just and free society required a long and difficult process. There was no magical, overnight solution. Revolutionists had to work hard and patiently, day by day, to peacefully convert the people, by rational argument, to the truths of social and economic justice. Only then would democratic freedom come.

Between Bakunin and Karl Marx (1818–83), as between Bakunin and Herzen, there was a lifelong struggle over ideas. In a letter, Bakunin said of Marx: "He wants what we want, the total triumph of economic and social equality. But . . ." That "but" divided the two revolutionaries. Bakunin pointed out that Marx wanted that triumph "through state power, through the dictatorship of a very strong and so to speak despotic government, which means through negation of freedom. His economic ideal is the state as the single owner of land and of any kind of capital."

Bakunin and his anarchist friends wanted to do away with the state. "We want the reconstruction of society not from above down, with the help of some kind of

authority . . . but from below up through the free fed-
eration of workers' associations, free from the yoke of
the state."

Marx, the German philosopher and radical leader,
was the chief theorist of modern socialism. In the *Communist Manifesto* of 1848, he and his friend Friedrich
Engels (1820–95) prophesied that communism would
triumph in Europe. (Today more than a third of the
world's population lives under governments professing
communism.) Marx urged the workers to seize the factories from the owners and place the means of production in the hands of the revolutionary government for
the benefit of all. That in-between society he called the
dictatorship of the proletariat, or working class. That
was to be only the first step, however. His theory promised that true communism would come with the next
step: the state giving ownership back to the people,
who would no longer need direction and control by a
ruling class of workers. But nowhere in the world has
this state of pure communism, this paradise on earth,
been achieved.

Did Marx view terrorism as a necessary tool, the way
Bakunin did? Marx believed in revolution, but not in
individual terror. He ridiculed Karl Heinzen's ideas,
and bitterly attacked Bakunin. True, at one time Marx
thought that the assassination of the tsar might be the
spark to ignite revolutionary fires all over Russia. But
he came to believe that political action was the only
sound way to revolution. He detested anarchism and
despised conspiratorial methods. He dismissed terror-

ism not on moral grounds, but because it was not effective.

As more and more acts of terrorism were reported in the following years, Marx labeled them "stupid," "silly," and "nonsensical." Such self-styled "heroic deeds," said Engels, were "pure Bakuninist bragging, purposeless propaganda by the deed."

Whatever Marx and Engels thought, Bakunin's influence on anarchism in Europe and America was great. This was more true in southern than in northern Europe. In the industrial states of northern Europe the workers relied on well-organized political parties and trade unions to improve their conditions. In more backward peasant societies, such as Italy and Spain, where progress was much harder to achieve, the belief in insurrection and terrorism took deeper root. Seeing no mass support for revolutionary change, the radicals in these places took up the idea of "propaganda by the deed." Only violent action, they said, would open the world's eyes to the desperation of the oppressed and the ruthless determination of those who wanted to end it.

Old and poor, ill and disillusioned by the failure of still another revolutionary project in Italy, Bakunin fled once more to Switzerland, where he died in exile.

Chapter 4

Sophia and the Tsar

On a Sunday morning in March 1881, the tsar of Russia was murdered by a band of terrorists.

In command of the killers was 27-year-old Sophia Perovskaya.

At fifteen Sophia was "as small as a gold coin," a friend had said, "but as precious." Blue eyes sparkled in a thin face, and her eager voice often gave way to infectious laughter. Her quick mind and deep curiosity made her an excellent student. She seemed to have every chance to enjoy the best of life, for she came from a family of aristocrats that had filled high office in Russian government. The dream of her father—the governor-general of St. Petersburg, the country's capital—was for his daughter to shine in high society.

But Sophia's vision was different. She shunned the

social life of her family's great country and town houses. She wanted not luxury and adoration, but equal rights for women and the education to help prepare her for that struggle. In her teens she entered a high school preparing girls for the university. There she met several other girls who shared her interest in the anarchist and socialist writings of the Russian radicals. Sophia joined with her classmates to form a women's study circle. They read forbidden books and discussed dangerous ideas. They were deeply troubled by the injustice they saw all around them. The imperial family that had ruled Russia for centuries cared nothing for the rights of man. The aristocracy—their own parents, in many cases— was lawless and brutal. The government was corrupt and disorganized. The masses lived in poverty. The need for reform was desperate. Educated Russians had formed movements to change the system of absolute monarchy; they hoped to put a republic in its place, or at least a constitutional monarchy. But the tsars gave not an inch: They kept iron control of Russia. Their spies were everywhere, sniffing out the faintest whiffs of dissent. True, Alexander II had introduced some reforms—he had, for example, freed the serfs in 1861. But that was a fraud. Forced to repay their owners, the serfs became enslaved to moneylenders instead of land-lords.

When a student tried to kill the tsar a few years later, the act gave the government the chance to put the brakes on reform. Liberalism had gone too far, the reaction-aries argued; anarchy threatened the regime. The tsar listened and cut reform dead. He expanded the secret police and clamped censorship tighter. Any talk of a constitution for Russia or of political freedoms was now a crime against the state. The police rounded up radicals and sentenced them to hard labor and imprisonment in Siberia. Many young people were sent into exile without trials. Dozens of political prisoners died of harsh treatment, committed suicide, or went insane in prison.

Sophia Perovskaya and her friends were drawn into the revolutionary movement. Most of its members were students from the universities, the technical schools, and the high schools. At first they believed the overthrow of tsarism would be simple and even bloodless. They merely had to bring the light to the "dark people," the peasants. Once shown their true interests, the peasants would make the revolution. For in these simple people were lodged true wisdom, goodness, and spirituality. The peasants—four fifths of the people of that vast land—were poor and largely illiterate, but the young idealists—often from the middle and upper classes— saw them as brothers and sisters. Together they would join in building a kingdom of heaven here on earth.

It was the year 1871 now, and Sophia Perovskaya was seventeen. The suspicious police kept a close eye on students, frightening some into shying away from danger. Not Sophia and her friends. The risks they took made their secret talks all the more intense.

Around them the young radicals saw men, women, and children sweated in the factories or on the huge estates often controlled by absentee landlords. The writings of Russian revolutionaries driven into exile were smuggled into the country, copied, and passed from hand to hand, feeding the hunger for a new faith and a new way of life.

Secret talk about revolution was fine, but when would they *do* something about their beliefs? And how? At first Sophia and her friends collected small bundles of political books and handed them to the factory workers of the capital. Their group and others like it were soon part of a network reaching into the provinces beyond the big cities.

Aware of his daughter's dangerous ideas, Sophia's father, an evil-tempered tyrant, demanded that she give up her foolish goals. When she refused, he slammed his door on her. It did not frighten Sophia to go out on her own. She was strong willed and passionately sure of her beliefs. She had the secret support of her mother, and the comradeship of young women who felt themselves joined together like a family.

That summer of 1871, Sophia's group joined with another to rent a house on the edge of St. Petersburg. Here they started a small commune for young men and women. Their aim was to learn to live simply, like the Russian poor. They pooled their funds and shared all housekeeping tasks. Women lived in one part of the house, men in another. Daily they did gymnastics in the yard to build their strength, and studied so that each in turn could give lectures in their seminar on socialism. Becoming perfect in body, mind, and spirit . . . only thus would they make themselves worthy of what they saw as their duty: to help oppressed people fight for truth and justice. They themselves—a privileged class—would not make the revolution; real changes in society, they believed, could be made only by the people themselves.

But how? What would be the right revolutionary policy for Russia? They debated theories, they argued about practical ways and means of making a revolution. First of all they had to mold themselves into an effective action group. They knew they all faced persecution, arrest, perhaps torture and execution. They must be able to trust each other absolutely. So at their meetings they talked openly of the character and behavior of each group member. They wanted no power-hungry leaders and no moral cowards in their movement.

By the end of that summer the group was as much a family as a political organization. What united them was not any radical dogma, but the intense power of their feelings.

They began their work of "going among the people." In the next few years they started mutual aid societies for workers, they gave a hand to the new trade unions, they opened schools for workers' children and adult education classes for parents. When victims of tsarism were arrested and exiled, they sent them packages and tried to organize their escape—and sometimes succeeded.

To avoid detection by the secret police and their spies, the young radicals carried false identity papers and dressed and looked like the laundresses, seamstresses, and factory workers they lived among. Sophia was especially good at impersonating a stupid-seeming peasant girl. She rented a tiny house near the Nevsky tollgate and pretended to be a housewife. There workers came to talk about the state of affairs in Russia, to learn to read and write, to study geography, history, science.

Since most of the peasants, on the other hand, could not read the revolutionary word, the radicals had to make them hear it. So in what became known as the "mad summer" of 1874, the radical groups took to the countryside. A famine had spread over huge regions of Russia, and the government had done nothing about it. Swept by a fever of idealism, thousands of young people spread through the stricken provinces to bring the peasants help and share their misery. Sophia's radical band with its supporting branches became the propaganda center of the movement to "go among the people."

Deep into Russia they went, expecting to find peasants waiting for the word to rise up against the tsar and seize the land. But the ex-serfs, though they lived in terrible poverty, were bound by deep religious faith to an almost instinctive loyalty to the tsar. They saw landlords and officials as their enemies, not the tsar. When the radicals came to preach revolutionary action, the peasants met them with suspicion and even hostility.

Alarmed by what their spies reported, the police arrested 1,600 of the young people, many of them between the ages of sixteen and twenty. About 200 were selected for trials, and 65 of them found guilty of joining an unlawful society to overthrow the government. Their sentences ran as high as ten years at hard labor.

The failure of the summer movement shook the faith of the young radicals. The disillusioned fell away, but the stronger, like Sophia's circle, did not abandon hope. Sophia too was arrested that summer, but she was allowed to await trial on her family's estate in the Crimea. Despotic as Russia was, its courts sometimes showed an independence that infuriated the tsar. Sophia's jury acquitted her, and fearing rearrest on some other charge, she went underground. For a year she tried to arrange the escape of her comrades, but failed. Arrested again in the Crimea, she escaped from her two guards while aboard the train to St. Petersburg. Said one of her comrades: "This small, graceful, ever-laughing young girl possessed a fearlessness that amazed the bravest of men."

Again—life in the underground, living under assumed names and with false identity papers. Now Sophia's circle was like a stricken family. Many were in prison or in exile. How could they work effectively? Mark Nathanson, medical student and a founder of Sophia's commune, escaped from exile and brought his passionate energy to reorganizing the scattered remnants of the radical groups. He pulled together a new secret society and revived the name of an old one for it: "Land and Freedom." With tighter control and stricter discipline they staged demonstrations in St. Petersburg. The police swiftly arrested many and gave them savage sentences. On appeal the tsar refused to reduce their prison terms and even increased some of them.

The old ways of working were no longer effective. Some of the radicals, burning with a desire for revenge, turned to terrorism. The first target was the St. Petersburg police chief, General Fedor Trepov, who had ordered the flogging of an imprisoned revolutionary for refusing to take off his cap when the chief passed. Vera Zasulich walked into Trepov's office and shot him, but failed to kill him. To the government's dismay, a jury acquitted her because of Trepov's reputation for brutality. She too disappeared underground.

Her act of terror, however, was a detonator for a gathering storm of violence. Soon there were more attempts on the lives of officials. The terrorists often resisted arrest and shot it out with the police who raided their hideouts. The chief of the tsar's secret police was himself assassinated.

The rising tide of terror caused a split in the Land and Freedom society. One group wanted to go on with propaganda work, trying to persuade the people to demand gradual reforms. The revolution would be justified only if it were the work of the people for whose benefit it was supposed to take place, they argued.

The others, impatient with the slow pace of education, frustrated with failure, formed an organization called The People's Will. Sophia chose to join this group. The long years of teaching, helping, organizing seemed wasted. Where was the peaceful change promised through education? How could they break through the tsar's repressive measures, the denial of freedom to speak, to publish, to organize? Didn't those barriers to success

justify the use of any means to achieve the one end—
revolution?

We do not know what inner struggle Sophia Perovskaya went through to come to the decision to use terror. Surely when she started out she had not wanted
violence. It would be terrible to take the life of another
human being. But even her women comrades were being
brutally beaten in prison. (One had just died of her
injuries, and another had gone insane.) Sophia saw herself as the bearer of the people's will. If the people
would not take action to help themselves, the enlight-
ened few must do it for them. And since the government
left no peaceful method open, terror was the only way.
Assassinate the leaders of government, the reasoning
went, and the regime would collapse, giving way to a
new and just order. It was not as hard to kill if you
thought of the victim not as a human being but as a
faceless abstraction—the symbol of tsarism.

As the wave of terror swept in, the tsar faced a political crisis. The liberal wing of the educated class urged
him to introduce reforms and even accept a constitutional government. The powerful ruling circle, however, thought the revolutionary danger was so great that
concessions would destroy the regime. Better to crush
the opposition with even more violence.

Russia plunged into a state of siege. Military officials
were given dictatorial powers and ordered to put down
sedition ruthlessly. The few radicals, knowing how weak
they were against the empire's giant power, had their
backs to the wall. They had to move fast to accomplish

their goal before the tsar could crush them. The tiny People's Will turned into a highly disciplined band of professional revolutionaries ready to function like a suicide squad. They had scarcely forty members, a third of them women. These, plus friends and sympathizers who would give them help, funds, and hiding places.

Sophia and Vera Figner became two of the leaders of the group. The other two were young men—Andrey Zhelyabov and Alexander Mikhalkov. It took them a year to shape their conspiratorial plans. In August of 1878 the group solemnly sentenced Tsar Alexander II to death.

Why the tsar? Because his feeble reforms had failed to bring political freedom to Russia. Posing as the patriarch of all the people, he had betrayed their confidence and love. The tsar himself was now the greatest barrier to change.

The conspirators believed no one else in the country—not the upper class, not the liberals, not the businessmen—had shown any intention of putting up a real fight for political freedom. If by some unpredictable means a democratic change should take place, then the revolutionaries would suspend their work and respect the will of the people. And should a revolution occur, The People's Will would never attempt to take it over and force "a despotic utopia" on the people. Their aim was only to destroy despotism, and there seemed now no other way to do it than to kill the tsar.

There was a sad lack of logic in this case for assassination. But bright as the young radicals were, they failed to see how circular their reasoning was. Here they were, launching plans to murder the tsar in the name of the people. Yet at the same moment they admitted that the people still believed in the tsar and would not rise up against him. Nevertheless the revolutionaries vowed again and again never to go against the will of the people!

Were they too obsessed with their aim to think clearly? Had they been so often disappointed and frustrated that their love for peace and decency and goodness had turned into blind hatred?

Eight times in the next eighteen months the terrorists attempted to carry out their sentence of death upon the tsar. They gave no thought to what might happen after the assassination. They made no preparation to seize power. Their only hope was that somehow the people would rise up and take their fate into their own hands.

Each of their plots required the most elaborate preparations. Almost all were aimed at killing the tsar while he moved about in his carriage or train. The first time, they mined the railroad tracks at Odessa, along the route the tsar took for his holidays in the Crimea. But he went by another route. The next time, the explosives were planted under the tracks at Alexandrovsk, but when the royal train went over them, nothing happened. The wiring was defective. The third attempt was in Moscow, where a tunnel to the tracks was dug from a house Sophia rented and a mine planted under the rails. But the explosion blew up the wrong train, not the one the tsar was riding.

By now all Russia knew terrorists were relentlessly hunting down the tsar. As Alexander himself said bitterly, "Am I such a wild beast that they should hound me to death?"

Late in 1879, four of the conspirators were arrested. They kept silent; the others went on trying to kill the tsar. One of them got himself hired as a carpenter to do some repair work in the Winter Palace. He managed to place dynamite under the floor of the tsar's dining room, setting the charge to go off as a state dinner was about to begin. The explosion occurred on schedule, but the tsar happened to be late that day. The victims were eleven guardsmen killed and 56 others wounded as the walls and floors caved in.

The morale of the court circle was shattered. Death had reached into the tsar's own home. St. Petersburg was placed under a state of siege. The public panicked, believing an army of terrorists roamed the city, capable of superhuman deeds. The tsar gave dictatorial powers to his minister of the interior and ordered him to root out the terrorists. The minister advised the tsar to make reforms. The violence, he said, erupted from the frustration of the people. They could not get anyone to listen to their grievances. All the tsar would agree to were some superficial gestures at reform—only enough to give the impression he was ready to let the people play some role in government.

But even as his advisers were drafting the changes, the terrorists were completing plans for another attempt. Sophia and a young man rented a shop along one of Odessa's main streets along which the tsar often rode. They dug a tunnel under the street, but while they were waiting for the delayed dynamite to arrive, the tsar came and went. Their next attempt was to mine a bridge in St. Petersburg that the tsar often crossed on the way to board his train. On the appointed day he did cross it, but one of the plotters failed to arrive on time to set the fuse. He didn't own a watch, he said.

Inefficient as the terrorists sometimes were, they could be outdone by the police. It would seem hard to conceal all these secret moves when police spies were everywhere. How could you make dynamite or bombs in a rented room and conceal the fumes and stink of chemicals? How could you operate a printing press without lots of noise where there wasn't even supposed to be one? How could you carry out bulky bundles of printed material without being noticed?

Still, long as it took, the police managed to grope their way to the heart of The People's Will. Several members were arrested and tried. Two were hanged and the others given long sentences at hard labor in the mines, or solitary confinement in fortresses. Meanwhile the survivors prepared for the next attempt upon the tsar. Early in 1881 Sophia and Zhelyabov, posing as cheese merchants, rented a shop in St. Petersburg and night after night mined their way beneath it to a point under the street where the tsar's carriage nearly always passed over on his way to observe the Sunday parade of troops. They chose March 1 as the day of execution.

Shortly before the fatal day things started to go wrong.

Neighbors of the "cheese merchants" had grown suspicious, and the police paid the shop a visit. They found nothing but a nice choice of cheeses, and a little dirt piled in a corner. Had they looked more closely, they would have uncovered the tunnel the plotters had dug.

Then there were more arrests, among them Zhelyabov. With the master plotter in prison, Sophia took command. One of the terrorists, a young chemist, had designed a new bomb that had to be thrown by hand from close to the victim. It meant the conspirators had little chance of escaping alive.

On March 1 Sophia, with two bombs on her lap, drove to her rendezvous with four terrorists. Two would be lookouts, two bomb throwers. The plotters went over their signals a last time, then moved to their stations. Sophia posted herself where she could see the royal sleigh's movements and signal her men to prepare for action.

She watched the tsar set out for the parade, but instead of going along the street where the mined tunnel had been dug, he drove by way of the Catherine Canal embankment parallel to it. Guessing he would return the same way, she placed the bomb throwers along the embankment. The tsar's sleigh raced back along the embankment, with six Cossack guards riding beside it and ahead, and two sleighs of police behind it. The first terrorist, Rysakov, a nineteen-year-old worker, saw Sophia's handkerchief signal, readied himself, and threw his bomb. But it fell just behind the tsar's sleigh. Flames shot up as the sound of the explosion shattered the

Sunday quiet. The back of the sleigh was torn apart. On the snow lay a wounded Cossack and a dying boy who had been passing by. The terrified horses dragged the sleigh another hundred yards before the driver was able to rein them in. The tsar got out unharmed and walked toward the bleeding figures in the snow, his officers failing to restrain him. As he came up to the spot where the bomb had burst, another of the terrorists, the nobleman Grinevitsky, leaned against a wall watching him. When the tsar was almost abreast of him, Grinevitsky flung a bomb at his feet. Stone, flesh, snow, blood, fire fountained high in the air. The bomb's roar faded, replaced by screaming. Then silence.

The tsar lay dying, blood from his many wounds staining the snow. Around him lay twenty others, dying in the street, Grinevitsky among them. Still alive, the tsar was rushed to the palace. He died an hour later.

The next day The People's Will issued a manifesto, taking responsibility for the murder:

> Alexander II, the tormentor of the people, has been put to death by us, Socialists. He was killed because he did not care for his people, burdened them with unauthorized taxes, deprived the peasants of their land and surrendered the workers to the mercy of plunderers and exploiters. He did not give the people freedom: he did not listen to their griefs and their tears. He defended only the rich and lived himself in the utmost luxury, while the people went hungry.
>
> The Tsar's servants, from the village police to the high officials, plundered the people and barbarously mal-

treated the peasants; and these servants of the Tsar were especially protected and rewarded by the Tsar. Those who stood out for the people he hanged or exiled to Siberia.

So he was killed. A Tsar should be a good shepherd, ready to lay down his life for his flock: Alexander II was a ravening wolf and a terrible death has struck him. Now a new Tsar, Alexander III, climbs to the throne. He must not be allowed to behave like his father. May he proceed to hold general elections in the villages and towns and in all the factories. May he recognize the sorrows and deep needs of the people, and go forward into the truth!

The terrorists had finally succeeded.

The tsar was dead.

But what did the assassination do for social justice or freedom?

Its result was only further repression and reaction.

The Russian people were stunned by the news. The workers did not rise up in the cities to seize power. The peasants thought Alexander had been assassinated by noblemen who wanted to restore serfdom. The students' only gesture was to refuse to contribute money for wreaths to honor the dead tsar.

Interrogation broke Rysakov down. He said he repented his part in the plot, and gave information. Most of the major plotters, including Sophia, were rounded up within ten days. Unlike Rysakov they stood by their beliefs. After a quick trial the prisoners were sentenced to be executed. They were hanged on gallows in the

The assassins of Tsar Alexander II, a moment before execution on the gallows in a public square in St. Petersburg. The woman's figure in the center is Sophia Perovskaya, a leader of the small band of terrorists called The People's Will.

public square, where 80,000 people gathered to watch them die.

Almost before their corpses were taken down, the new tsar, Alexander III, announced the end of all reforms. In place of a constitution, he gave dictatorial power over the citizenry to all his governors. For his chief adviser he chose a fanatical reactionary who believed in a police state. Within two weeks of the executions pogroms against the Jews exploded in over 160 cities and villages of Southeast Russia. The controlled press had suggested that Jews were behind the assassination. Police terror would dominate civil life for decades to come.

About six months after Sophia and the others were executed, the news came that the president of the United States, James A. Garfield, had been assassinated. Whoever was left in The People's Will addressed an open letter to the American people. After voicing sorrow at Garfield's death, the letter went on to denounce the use of political murder in America:

> In a country in which the freedom of the individual allows an honest contest of ideas, where the will of the people determines not only the forms of law but the actual persons of the rulers—in such a country political murder is an expression of the same despotic spirit which we feel it our duty to combat in Russia. Despotism, whether of a person or a party, is always reprehensible, and violence is justifiable only when it is directed against violence.

Chapter 5

Bombs in Their Baggage

The tsar's death at the hands of the Russian terrorists opened an era of political bombings and assassinations. Most of these deeds were credited to anarchists, although many of the movement's leaders denounced them. One reason was that Italian anarchists traveled much in Europe and America, giving the impression that they were central to an international conspiracy of terror. Then too, whether or not anarchists were guilty of the violence, they often praised the assassins.

The calendar of major assassinations in this period:

> *1894*—President Sadi Carnot of France is murdered in Lyons by an Italian anarchist using a knife.

> *1897*—The Prime Minister of Spain, Cánovas del Castillo, is assassinated by an Italian anarchist.

1898—Elisabeth, Empress of Austria and Queen of Hungary, is stabbed to death by an Italian anarchist.

1900—King Umberto I of Italy is killed by an Italian anarchist.

1908—King Carlos I of Portugal and his heir apparent, Prince Luis Felipe, are slain in Lisbon by two members of a secret political society.

1911—Prime Minister Pyotr Stolypin of Russia is killed in Kiev by a member of the Socialist Revolutionary Party.

1914—Archduke Franz Ferdinand, nephew and heir of the Austro-Hungarian Emperor Franz Joseph II, is assassinated, along with his wife Sophia, by a young Serb nationalist. The murder sets in motion a chain of events that precipitates World War I.

In Italy "propaganda by the deed" emerged in the 1870s as the gospel of the revolutionary movement. The anarchists had sizeable popular support in a country with the revolutionary tradition of Mazzini and Garibaldi who had fought for Italy's freedom and were now in their old age. To rival those earlier heroes the new generation felt it had to carry out uprisings throughout Italy. Bologna was the first target, but troops dispersed the handful of rebels, and an alerted police force foiled the plots in other cities.

Perhaps as a result of frustration, individual acts of terrorism began to occur. The anarchist press called for the killing of "all kings, emperors, presidents of republics, priests of all religions," as "true enemies of the people." On a November day in 1878 a cook jumped onto the carriage of the new King Umberto in Naples and tried to stab him with a knife. The next day a bomb was hurled into a monarchist parade in Florence and four people were killed. Two days later a bomb exploded among a crowd of people in Pisa, but no one was killed. Within a month, all the known militant anarchists were in prison or in exile.

For another 25 years Italian anarchist activity was mainly the work of a few individuals. The small groups disappeared under police pressure, and like many other Italians, anarchists too chose emigration as the way to a better life. Going abroad to live, they carried their revolutionary ideas in their baggage. In the Middle East, in Latin America, in the United States, the major missionaries of anarchism were Italian immigrants. Their name was blackened by the work of Italian assassins who, as we have seen, were often the self-appointed executioners of heads of state.

Most Italian anarchists were neither assassins nor terrorists. They agitated for revolutionary change while they lived hand to mouth either at home or abroad. One of their earliest leaders, Andrea Costa, left anarchism and helped found the Italian Socialist Party. He repudiated terrorist plots as immoral and useless:

By means of a conspiracy, a change in the form of government can be obtained; a principle can be dispossessed or punctured and another put in its place, but it cannot achieve social revolution. . . . To do this is a matter of widely diffusing the new principles to the masses . . . so that the revolution occurs by itself from the bottom to the top and not vice versa. . . . And this necessarily involves publicity, since it is impossible to reconcile the idea of such a vast propaganda within the necessarily restricted circle of a conspiracy.

When such advice was ignored, the results were tragic. Terrorists carried on as a small minority among Italian anarchists. After a wave of strikes in Italy ended in defeat in 1920, disappointed terrorists in Milan planted bombs in a theater, a power station, and a hotel. Twenty-one people were killed and many more injured. The violence did great harm to the reputation of anarchists among all classes, including the workers. It gave Mussolini's Fascists an excuse for counterviolence against the left. The right-wing terror spread, helping to bring Mussolini to power.

Anarchism was taken up in the Spain of the nineteenth century with the fervor of a new religion, and it has endured there ever since. The first of all anarchist journals appeared in Spain as early as 1845. The major movement, however, did not start until the revolution of 1868 drove Queen Isabella II into exile. Then Bakunin sent into Spain disciples who recruited lifelong leaders of anarchism. The movement flourished among both the peasants of the south and the workers of the north.

A more violent era opened in 1878, when a young worker tried to kill King Alfonso XII. Mass arrests followed, then protest strikes and more government repression. One wing of the anarchist movement chose to form its own terrorist organization, The Disinherited, and called for random assassinations. It gave the civil guard an excuse to crush the movement. When a tavernkeeper suspected of being a police informer was murdered by villagers, the civil guard blamed it on what they claimed was a huge secret society, the Black Hand. Using informers and torture, the police netted all the active anarchists and garroted seven of them in the public square. No one has ever proved the Black Hand really existed, although there were small terrorist groups in the district.

In the early 1890s Spain saw a sudden outburst of bombings and assassinations, as widespread as an epidemic. Some of it was the work of anarchists, and some the provocation of police agents. Soon some employers hired gunmen to fight it out on the streets with the anarchists. When one young anarchist, who had thrown a bomb that missed its target, was caught and executed, his friend took terrible revenge: He tossed a bomb into a fashionable theater and killed twenty people. The government took advantage of the public's horrified revulsion to round up all the anarchist leaders they could find, and executed several of them who were obviously innocent.

Again, a vicious circle. The police violence led to more bombings and shootings, then more arrests, then more torture, and finally the bombing of a Corpus Christi procession in Barcelona in 1896. The bomb killed only workingmen and women, and was thought to be the work of the police, who collared 400 opponents of the regime and the Church and put them to such grisly torture that several died before trial. In the end 26 got long prison terms, and five were executed, without any proof of guilt. It was to avenge that horror that Spain's prime minister of the time, Cánovas, was murdered by an Italian anarchist.

In France, too, terrorism spread like an epidemic. Between 1892 and 1894 there were a dozen major acts of violence. Several of the terrorists called their outrages "acts of propaganda by the deed." One of the terrorists became a legendary figure in the anarchist movement. He was François Claudius Ravachol. Abandoned in childhood by his father, he survived on odd jobs. And petty thievery, liquor smuggling, and counterfeiting. Gaining little from these, he turned to shockingly violent crimes. He murdered an old ragpicker, and then an old hermit, whose savings he stole, and finally two old women keeping a small shop. Arrested, Ravachol escaped and went to Paris. There, after reading anarchist papers that printed articles on "chemistry in the home," he picked up the tools and materials needed to make bombs in his kitchen.

His first terrorist plot—and it proved to be his last—was an act of revenge against judges who had just sentenced workers for taking part in a May Day demonstration. (May Day—May 1—is the traditional European Labor Day, and leftists as well as trade unionists use it as "their" day for demonstrations.) Ravachol planted bombs in two apartment blocks where the judges lived. But his clumsy work damaged only the buildings without killing anyone. Going off to a restaurant immediately afterwards, Ravachol tried to convert his waiter to anarchism. The man reported him to the police, who arrested him for the bombings. The day after Ravachol's trial began, the restaurant was wrecked by a bomb and the owner, but not the waiter, killed. The jury found Ravachol guilty of the bombings and sentenced him to hard labor for life. The authorities then put him on trial for his earlier crime of killing the hermit. When sentenced to death, he shouted, "Long live anarchy!" After Ravachol's execution he was called a martyr and a saint by the anarchists. Ballads were written about him and his name became a verb—*ravacholiser*: to blow up.

Different from Ravachol in temperament and background was the anarchist Emile Henry. This brilliant young man came from a middle-class family. When converted to anarchism, he quit school to plot propaganda by the deed. His first terrorist attack, with his own homemade bomb, was on the Paris offices of a mining company. It had just brutally smashed a strike in its coalfields. The police discovered the bomb before it went off, but it exploded in their stationhouse and killed five officers.

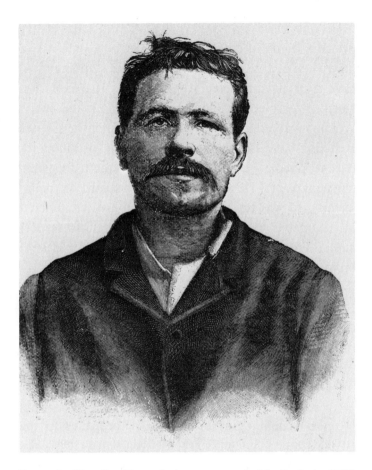

François Claudius Ravachol was executed in Paris in 1892 for brutal murders and bombings. After his death the anarchists created a legend about him as a revolutionary martyr.

No one knew who was guilty. A year later Henry placed a bomb in a café next to a railway station at a time when a large crowd of people were stopping by to have a drink and listen to the band. The explosion wrecked the place, wounded twenty, and killed one.

Henry was caught and tried. During his trial he showed a chilling hatred of society. Reproached for killing innocent people, he replied, "They aren't the only innocent ones." He stood up to tell the court the bomb in the café was his reprisal for the injustices inflicted by bourgeois society. Why should anarchists respect human life when the upper classes did not? He went on to say:

> Anarchists do not spare bourgeois women and children, because the wives and children of those they love are not spared either. Are not those children innocent victims who, in the slums, die slowly of anemia because bread is scarce at home: or those women who grow pale in your workshops and wear themselves out to earn 40 sous a day, and yet are lucky when poverty does not turn them into prostitutes; those old people whom you have turned into machines for production all their lives, and whom you cast on the garbage dump and the workhouse when their strength is exhausted? At least have the courage of your crimes, gentlemen of the bourgeoisie, and agree that our reprisals are fully legitimate!

While some terrorists planned acts of revenge against specific individuals or representatives of a class, others attempted symbolic acts of self-destruction that would at the same time destroy the symbols of the state. Such a deed was Auguste Vaillant's. A joiner of radical groups, he discovered anarchism and decided to kill himself by a final gesture that would speak for all the victims of society. In his room he prepared a powerful bomb designed to scatter projectiles widely. He sneaked it into the Chamber of Deputies and hurled it from a balcony. When the echoes of the tremendous explosion faded and the smoke cleared, there was blood and debris everywhere. Somehow no one was killed. Vaillant was tried and executed, proclaiming with his last breath, "Long live anarchy! My death will be avenged!"

In six months, it was. Sadi Carnot, the French president who had refused clemency for Vaillant, was stabbed to death while visiting in Lyons. The assassin was a 21-year-old Italian anarchist. It was the rapid succession of murders that helped shape the popular image of the bearded anarchist with smoking bomb in one hand and dripping dagger in the other. Ordinary criminals, too, soon began to claim they were anarchists simply trying to right the wrongs of the social order. Their thieving was a means of redistributing the wealth, said these newborn Robin Hoods.

And distinguished men of otherwise high principle, convinced of the immorality of property, were ready to justify theft of any kind on much the same ground. Among them were many of France's intellectuals and artists. Early in the 1890s they began to identify themselves with anarchism. For some it became fashionable to be seen at least on the fringes of the radical movement, much as it would in the 1960s and '70s in New

York, San Francisco, London, Paris, Berlin. Camille Pissarro (1830–1903) was only one of the many important French painters intimately linked to anarchism, contributing his work to its journals. And so too were famous novelists, poets, dramatists. Anarchism represented to them liberation from worn-out social, moral, and artistic bonds. Its stress on the spirit of inquiry, on independence of thought, on freedom of action, appealed to them. Even when the sensational bombings and assassinations occurred, many artists and intellectuals were not repelled. While *they* might not move from talk to violence, they applauded the terrorists for doing so. The very sensationalism of terrorist life intrigued them. That was why it was possible for so appalling a criminal as Ravachol to be hailed as a martyr.

As for the French terrorists of the 1890s, their crimes cannot be blamed on any organized movement. None of the assassins belonged to a disciplined group, as had Sophia Perovskaya and her comrades of The People's Will. They took orders from no one, but planned their murders on their own initiative. They saw themselves as judges and executioners, but the world looked upon them as criminals. Their violent actions, done in the name of anarchism, did not advance that cause one inch nor lighten the weight of injustice for a single soul. As one French commentator said, "Every party has its criminals and its fools, because every party has its men."

Chapter 6

Terrorism, American Style

Was America safe from terrorism?

Almost as the last guns of the Civil War were silenced, an underground army of white terrorists began an attack upon the new democracy of the South. Within a dozen years they succeeded in disenfranchising more than half the population below the Mason-Dixon line.

The Ku Klux Klan was the chief instrument of the terrorists. It was founded by young ex-Confederate soldiers in 1865, at the end of the war. The name was invented because it sounded strange, and to deepen the mystery the members wore weird costumes—white masks, high conical hats, long flowing robes. They met and moved in secrecy and appeared as members in public only in their white disguise.

The Klan spread with amazing speed throughout the

The Ku Klux Klan, a secret terrorist society flourishing in the South during the Reconstruction period, as seen by Thomas Nast, the political cartoonist. The KKK, seeking to restore white Democratic rule, intimidated and murdered black voters who supported the Republican Party.

South. By 1867 there were hundreds of local units. Under the command of Grand Dragon Nathan B. Forrest they called themselves an "Invisible Empire." Forrest had been a Confederate cavalry general and, before the war, a rich slave trader. He bragged of having half a million members, all armed, and "opposed to Negro suffrage under any and all circumstances."

The slaveholders' rebellion had been crushed and the black slaves liberated by the victory of Union arms. The new Thirteenth, Fourteenth, and Fifteenth Amendments to the Constitution had outlawed slavery forever, made Blacks citizens, and given black males the vote. It was a great leap forward for American democracy. For the first time in Southern history black men joined with poor whites to write new state constitutions. Both now had the right to vote or hold office without owning property. Free schooling was open to all. Reform after reform was adopted as the newly chosen legislators acted on behalf of the majority's social and economic needs.

It was the new political power of the poor and the black that moved the Klan to use terror to smash what was called Reconstruction. The Klan and several other secret organizations combined their forces to restore white supremacy to the South. This was not a struggle between armies. The Civil War had just ended, costing both sides enormous losses in life and property. No one wanted it to start up again. The North was reluctant to mass troops in great numbers to restore law and order. And the ex-rebels wished to avoid head-on battles that would inevitably bring their defeat.

The method the enemies of Reconstruction chose was terrorism. They turned to the lash, the torch, the noose, and the gun. Blacks and whites who tried to teach the freedmen their political rights, who tried to help them to vote, who preached black-white equality, were their targets.

In Georgia alone, in 1868, there were 336 cases of murder or attempted murder of Blacks by the Klan. Hundreds of beatings were reported, the victims lashed 300 to 500 times each. Georgia, said the KKK, must be a white man's state, and it swore to persecute any leaders of the Blacks mercilessly.

For four years Mississippi saw the Klan ride through the countryside at night, terrifying, whipping, or murdering whites and Blacks they didn't like. "Roving gangs of terrorists," wrote the historian Vernon L. Wharton,

> murdered respectable Negro preachers, drove off and killed Negro renters of land, rifled stores and took the lives of Jewish merchants, lynched Negro men, women and children who were accused of vague crimes, and killed or robbed peaceful white citizens.

The terrorist bands operated on their own, many under the Klan's name, others using different names. But all were united in the common goal of enforcing white supremacy. Most of the Klan leaders came from the well-to-do white class. The rank and file were from all classes, from high society to illiterate poor whites. As the beatings and killings multiplied, the dominant whites denied any responsibility. It was "bad people" who had sneaked into the Klan, taken over, and given it a nasty name, they said. No one believed that. "As between the upper and lower classes," wrote the Klan historian Allen W. Trelease, "it would be difficult to assign the greater guilt for the atrocities which took place in the name of white supremacy."

Why wasn't the Klan stopped? Weren't there laws, courts, police in the South? Backed by those in power, the local Klans had little to fear. They moved in secrecy, true, but their chief protection was their friends in high places. Even when their identities became known, Klansmen rarely were punished. Other Klansmen stood ready to give them false alibis, frighten witnesses and officials, pressure juries. A handful were brought to the bar of justice; even fewer were convicted.

The story of Alonzo B. Corliss shows how the system worked. A white northerner, partially crippled, he had come down to Alamance County, North Carolina, to teach in a Quaker-supported school for Blacks. He became head of a political club of black and white Republicans. The Klan hated what he was doing. They raided his home, hauled him into the woods, and gave him thirty lashes. They shaved one side of his head, painted it black, and warned him to leave the county. Corliss had guts; he stayed put. His landlord then kicked him out of his house and no one else would rent him a room. When Corliss had four of the raiders arrested, the law refused to prosecute them.

Wherever the Klan operated, it aimed to halt public schooling. But education was what the Blacks wanted more than anything else. Because it had been illegal in many states to teach Blacks to read, the illiteracy rate for Southern Blacks under slavery was 95 percent. (Whites had had no public schools either except in North Carolina.) As every foot of Southern territory was taken over by the Union armies, abolitionists and missionaries came in to offer education to the Blacks. The freed people started their own schools, too. Classrooms held blacks of all ages, so eager was everyone to learn. To be able to read and write was to be truly free and independent.

But for the Southern whites education for Blacks was the devil himself. They had always forbidden it and now they fought it bitterly. Lumber merchants would not supply wood for black schools and carpenters would not build them. White and black women from the North who volunteered to teach Blacks were called "prostitutes" and "nigger teachers." Black pupils were beaten up, classroom windows were smashed, schoolhouses were burned down. If teachers stuck to their jobs, they were publicly whipped or even murdered.

The Republicans had taken control of the country and had made their party strong in the South by giving the vote to Blacks and winning their loyalty. They placed some troops in the South to protect the freedmen from the old slaveholders. But they were too few and too scattered to prevent the widespread terror. Most of the white community backed the Klan. If Blacks would not vote their way, Klansmen blocked them from the polls or threw out their ballots. When Blacks fought back, the Klan whipped them, or burned their crops, barns, and homes.

Nevertheless, for a time democracy did manage to advance in the South. During the ten brief years of Reconstruction Blacks held almost every kind of office in town, county, and state governments, and some sat in the halls of Congress. At every level they had the powerful opposition of white Democrats to contend with. And of course there were white Republicans who did not wish to share power with them.

Even though the Blacks never sought racial domination, but only equality, the whites never let up on their terror. It grew so great that by 1871 Congress passed laws to crush the secret societies. Although hundreds of terrorists were arrested, tried, and convicted, the terror went on. The Kluxers would not give up the fight to restore white rule. As Blacks began to ask for positions of political leadership in proportion to their numbers, the white Republicans drew away. Many dropped out of the party, and the freedmen found themselves nearly alone.

In state after state the Democratic party returned to power through terror and the threat of terror. At the same time the support the North had once given Blacks faded away. When the old abolitionist congressional leaders died, new Republicans showed more interest in money and business than in racial equality or civil rights. Then came the closely contested presidential election of 1876. With the outcome in doubt, a political deal was made between the two parties. It ended Reconstruction. The Republicans got the Presidency in return for a promise to remove federal troops from the South. In 1877 President Rutherford B. Hayes took office in Washington, while the white-supremacist Democrats returned to full rule in the South.

For nearly a century to come Southern Blacks would remain effectively without a vote and without a voice in a government that called itself a democracy. It is the best—or worst—American example of how effective political terrorism on a mass scale can be.

The Ku Klux Klan was terrorism, American style. Another form of terrorism was imported from abroad a few years after Reconstruction ended. In 1882 a German radical landed in New York to spread "propaganda by the deed." Johann Most was in his mid-thirties, a little man with gruff voice, twisted jaw hidden by a beard, and bitter eyes. A bookbinder by trade, he had joined the German Socialist party. The socialists believed that the only sound way to revolution was through an educated mass movement of workers winning control of the state. Johann Most rose to prominence in the party because of his fiery intelligence and passionate oratory. Converted to anarchism and the immediate destruction of the old order, Most was twice elected to the Reichstag—the German parliament—but was forced to flee when Germany adopted strict antisocialist laws. In London in 1879 he founded and edited the weekly *Freiheit* (Freedom), which called for the use of terrorism to overthrow the governments of Europe and America.

The British offered political exiles the freedom to

publish what they wished so long as they did not put their ideas into practice. But when Sophia Perovskaya's bomb throwers succeeded in killing the tsar, Most went beyond the limits. His editorial in *Freiheit* applauded the assassination with such joy, it embarrassed Britain's relations with Russia, and Most was sent to prison for eighteen months.

Even with the editor jailed, Britain let *Freiheit* go on. Until, that is, another editorial hailed the Irish assassins of two Englishmen as heroes. The paper was suppressed. When released from prison, Most sailed for New York to reestablish *Freiheit* there for the many German workers and craftsmen who had emigrated to America. He arrived at one of the most turbulent times in American history. Conflicts between capital and labor had reached a new pitch of open warfare with the great railroad strike of 1877. It had led to riots in a dozen cities that caused death to ninety and injuries to thousands of others. Battles between workers and the employers' armies of hired gunmen were almost too much for the police and the military to control. The middle and upper classes were panicked into the mistaken belief that a national insurrection was about to take place.

Most's message to the brutally mistreated and underpaid workers (a great many of them immigrants) was to rush to revolution. Only violence, the bomb, could free them from oppression, he preached. Dynamite alone would destroy both the plutocrats and the government that furnished them with troops and guns to put down the working class.

With his vivid personality and his dramatic history as a political prisoner, Most was greeted here as a revolutionary hero. He quickly became the leader of the most militant radicals. Within a few years of his arrival there were some 7,000 American anarchists organized in eighty groups. Chicago alone had about 2,000 anarchists, some with ties to local trade unions. Most toured American cities to deliver a series of lectures on anarchism and the use of terrorist tactics. Under his influence Chicago's socialist paper, the *Arbeiter Zeitung*, turned anarchist and flourished appeals to violence.

On April 5, 1885:

> Here is something worth hearing. A number of strikers in Quincy [Illinois], yesterday, fired upon their bosses, and not upon the scabs. This is recommended most emphatically, for imitation.

On May 5, 1885:

> Workmen ought to take aim at every member of the militia, and do with him as one would do with someone of whom it is known that he is after taking one's life. It might sooner be difficult to obtain murdering tools. . . . Workmen, arm yourselves!

And on February 21, 1885, in *Alarm*, the Chicago paper of the anarchist Albert Parsons:

> Dynamite! Of all the good stuff, that is the stuff! Stuff several pounds of this sublime stuff into an inch pipe (gas or water pipe), plug up both ends, insert a cap with a fuse attached, place this in the immediate vicinity of

a lot of rich loafers who live by the sweat of other people's brows, and light the fuse. A most cheerful and gratifying result will follow. . . . The dear stuff . . . is a genuine boon for the disinherited, while it brings terror and fear to the robbers. A pound of this good stuff beats a bushel of ballots all hollow—and don't you forget it!

Johann Most decided it was not enough to call for the use of dynamite and the bomb: He must teach the workers how to make and use those weapons. So under a false name he took a job in a New Jersey explosives factory and used what he learned to publish a remarkable handbook for terrorists called *The Science of Revolutionary Warfare*. In it (and in articles in *Freiheit*) he described how to make bombs, how to break into public buildings, how to commit burglary and arson, how to obtain and use poisons against the enemies of labor and the revolution. It was a do-it-yourself manual that would have delighted Nechayev, and it was widely read.

Most's influence was strongest perhaps in Chicago, which was the most radical city in the country in the 1870s and '80s. Anarchist leaders now dominated the Central Labor Union there to the extent that resolutions were adopted with such appeals as this:

We urgently call upon the wage class to arm itself in order to put forth against their exploiters such an argument as alone can be effective—*Violence!*

This was 1886, and the Central Labor Union was fighting to win an eight-hour day for the workers of Chicago. Going on strike for the demands, the unions

Johann Most preaching to American audiences that only the bomb could free the working class from oppression. Exiled from Germany, he became a leader of militant radicals in the U.S. and published a handbook for terrorists.

were met with violent assaults by police and armed strikebreakers. One of the city's largest employers, the McCormick Harvesting Machine Company, locked out its striking workers and hired a few hundred gunmen supplied by the Pinkerton National Detective Agency—to terrorize them.

On May 3 the police clashed with the striking workers at the McCormick plant, killing four and wounding several others. A meeting to protest police brutality was called by the labor unions for the next night in Haymarket Square. About ten P.M., when the last speaker was winding down, 180 police suddenly marched into the peaceful square. Their commander ordered the workers to disperse. Suddenly, out of nowhere, a dynamite bomb exploded, killing seven police and wounding 67 others. In the dark the police fired into the crowd. In a few seconds the square was red with blood. Ten workers fell dead and another fifty were wounded.

The next day newspapers in Chicago and around the nation screamed for revenge. It was instantly decided, without any proof, that the bomb was the work of anarchists. The police arrested hundreds of anarchists at random. Eight were tried for conspiracy to murder and convicted. No proof was offered that any of the eight had planted or thrown a bomb. Nor was it proved that the speakers at the meeting had incited to violence. After the mockery called a trial, four of the innocent men were hanged. Seven years later, Governor of Illinois John Peter Altgeld investigated the Haymarket affair and courageously declared it to be a barefaced

A pamphlet aimed at the anarchists accused of the Haymarket bombing in Chicago in 1886. Years later the Illinois governor called the trial of the anarchists a mockery and pardoned the three men still in prison.

judicial murder. When he pardoned the three men still in prison (the fourth had killed himself), Altgeld became the most hated man in America.

Appeals for terror and terror itself had produced not progress, only counterterror. Johann Most and his followers made anarchism anathema in America.

Six years after the Haymarket bomb, one of Johann Most's disciples, Alexander Berkman, attempted the assassination of one of America's leading industrialists. It happened in 1892, when Andrew Carnegie and his chief aide, Henry Clay Frick, were using every weapon at their command to reduce wages and oust the union in their steel mill at Homestead, Pennsylvania. Acting for Carnegie, Frick had demanded that the workers accept a wage cut of 18 to 26 percent. The workers could see no reason for it. Times were good; Carnegie's dozen plants around Pittsburgh were filling his pockets with untaxed profits of 2 to 20 million dollars a year. At Homestead the Iron and Steel Workers craft union had organized the 800 skilled workers. But it had turned its back on the other 3,000 workers, most of them unskilled and recent arrivals from eastern Europe.

Carnegie decided this was the moment to break the craft union and make the whole plant nonunion. When the workers refused to take a wage cut, Frick shut down the mill and locked out the workers. Then he hired 300 Pinkertons to come into the plant so they could protect the scabs he meant to hire.

On July 6 at dawn, barges carrying the Pinkertons reached the plant landing on the river and tried to disembark the armed men. But the workers saw this invasion as the attempt of an unauthorized armed force to subjugate them. They were waiting with shotguns, pistols, clubs, and stones. They shouted to the barges to turn back, but the Pinkertons started down the gangplank for the shore. Firing broke out on both sides, and for thirteen hours the battle raged, one of the bloodiest in American labor history. Some twenty Pinkertons and forty strikers were shot. Seven Pinkertons and nine strikers died. At five P.M. the Pinkertons raised a white flag and came ashore unarmed, where the enraged wives of the strikers beat them badly before the police stopped them.

News of bloody Homestead shook the outside world. Unions sent messages of support and contributions for the strike fund. Reading the headlines, two young anarchist followers of Johann Most decided that this was the time for propaganda by the deed. They would assassinate Frick and galvanize the workers to revolt.

Alexander Berkman, a dark, intense 21-year-old, came of a prosperous Russian-Jewish family. As a schoolboy in St. Petersburg he had prepared himself for the life of "a true revolutionist." At eighteen he had emigrated to New York, where he met Emma Goldman. Two years older than "Sasha," she was barely five feet tall, with a turned-up nose and expressive, blue-gray eyes. She too had been schooled in St. Petersburg, where she met young radicals and modeled herself on the legendary Sophia Perovskaya. At fifteen she had come to America and found work in a garment factory. On their

EMMA GOLDMAN IN 1892

ALEXANDER BERKMAN.

Emma Goldman and Alexander Berkman, young lovers and anarchists inspired by Johann Most, plotted to assassinate Henry Clay Frick, the steel magnate, for his brutality against the Homestead strikers. Berkman failed to kill Frick and served a long prison term.

first date Sasha and Emma had gone to hear Johann Most lecture. His speech was a passionate outcry against these responsible for the recent Haymarket tragedy and the execution of the Chicago anarchists. Recalling that night, Goldman wrote:

> He spoke eloquently and picturesquely. As if by magic, his disfigurement disappeared, his lack of physical distinction was forgotten. He seemed transformed into some primitive power, radiating hatred and love, strength and inspiration. The rapid current of his speech, the music of his voice, and his sparkling wit, all combined to produce an effect almost overwhelming. He stirred me to my depths.

Yet something about this and other speeches she heard him give troubled her:

> His call to extermination . . . Most was an idealist, yet he urged extermination. Could idealists be cruel? The enemies of life and joy and beauty are cruel. They are relentless, they have killed our great comrades. But must we, too, exterminate?

Most's ideas had a strong influence on Goldman. For a brief time they were lovers. It was he who induced her to take to the public platform and lecture on anarchism, a step that transformed her life. Now, enraged by Frick's brutality in the Homestead strike, she and Sasha planned a supreme deed to further their cause. Sasha was willing to give his life in the attempt to kill Frick, and though Emma begged to die with him, he insisted she should live on to explain its meaning to the workers.

While Sasha experimented with bombs in their tenement, Emma stood guard, dreading that a mistake might blow up the innocent families in the crowded house. But didn't the end justify the means?

> Our end was the sacred cause of the oppressed and exploited people. It was for them that we were going to give our lives. What if a few should have to perish? The many would be made free and could live in beauty and in comfort. Yes, the end in this case justified the means.

Berkman tested one of his two homemade bombs on Staten Island. It failed to go off. Probably the other one would fail, too. They decided on a gun instead, and raised the few dollars needed to buy the weapon and a train ticket to Pittsburgh. On July 23 Berkman burst into Frick's office, where he saw three men seated at a table. "Frick?" he asked of the black-bearded man whose picture he had studied. And as Frick rose, he fired three shots at him. When he saw the fallen Frick was not dead, he stabbed him twice with a dagger. Berkman was wrestled to the floor and turned over to the police.

Frick survived his multiple wounds. Berkman's trial was a hasty formality. He tried at the end to read the speech in defense of his act that he had prepared behind bars. But it was in German, and the translator bumbled so badly that the judge soon cut him off. The young anarchist was given a sentence of 22 years. (He served fourteen of them.)

Berkman was of course guilty of trying to murder

Frick. He did it to destroy Frick and spread anarchist propaganda. He failed to achieve either goal. Frick lived on to become an even harsher enemy of labor. As for any effect the deed had upon the workers, they would have no part of anarchism. They felt Berkman had interfered in *their* business and only harmed their cause. (They lost the strike. The union was broken throughout the steel industry.) American workers everywhere felt the same. And the public did not believe that Berkman meant his deed as a moral gesture in their behalf: They thought he must have done it for personal gain.

Not only did the public and the workers denounce Berkman. Even Johann Most turned against him. At the time of Berkman's attack upon Frick, Most had just been released from a year in prison—for a speech about the execution of the Haymarket martyrs. Right after Berkman's act Most said publicly that the attempt on Frick's life was a fake, a staged happening. Either the newspapers had rigged it with Berkman, or Berkman was just a nut, or maybe even one of Frick's hirelings, paid to do it to win sympathy for the steel master.

It was a complete reversal of Most's position. Goldman was enraged by this personal attack upon Sasha. After years of urging the supreme value of propaganda by the deed, and just when Berkman was being reviled by everyone for doing what Most called for, Most himself now declared he had misjudged the value of terrorism. It didn't make sense, he said, in a country with so small and weak a revolutionary movement.

Was Most scared to go back to prison? Goldman

wondered if he feared the press would accuse him of complicity in Sasha's deed. Or was he poisonously jealous of her love for Sasha? Emma branded Most a traitor and a coward, and demanded an explanation. When he did not respond, she appeared at his next lecture and from the front row again challenged him to prove his accusations. When he dismissed her as a "hysterical woman," she leaped onto the platform, pulled out a concealed whip, and repeatedly lashed him across the face and neck. Then she broke the whip across her knee and flung the pieces at him. It happened so fast no one had a chance to interfere. She and Most were never reconciled.

But Goldman too came to change her mind about terrorism. Years later she regretted that attempt on Frick's life:

> I feel violence in whatever form never has and probably never will bring constructive results. . . . Never again had I anything directly to do with an act of violence. . . . In the zeal of fanaticism I had believed that the end justifies the means. It took years of experience and suffering to emancipate myself from the mad idea. . . . I could never again participate in or approve of methods that jeopardized innocent lives.

Of assassination and terror there was more to come, both in America and abroad. In the half century between Lincoln's murder in 1865 and the murder of Archduke Franz Ferdinand in 1914, one head of state or major minister was killed nearly every eighteen months. President James Garfield was murdered by Charles Guiteau in 1881, but that was the act of a discontented office seeker, not a political terrorist. Twenty years later President William McKinley was shot by Leon Czolgosz, a young American of Polish descent. A factory worker, he had begun reading about anarchism while out on strike. The assassination of King Umberto I of Italy in 1900 fascinated him and he kept studying his clippings of the press accounts. In May of 1901 he heard a lecture by Emma Goldman on anarchism and soon after visited an anarchist club, dropping vague hints of terrorist plans. In Buffalo on September 6 he joined a line to shake hands with the president, who was visiting the Pan-American Exposition. When he reached McKinley, he fired a concealed pistol through his handkerchief. The president died eight days later. In a trial that lasted eight hours Czolgosz was found guilty. When he was strapped to the electric chair, he said, "I killed the president because he was the enemy of the good people—the working people. I am not sorry for my crime."

No proof ever came that the assassin was an agent of the anarchists or any other group. He was a loner who had suffered a nervous breakdown three years before and emerged an agitated potential killer with delusions that he was an anarchist with a duty to kill the president. And as with Berkman's shooting of Frick, nothing good came of it. The crime provoked a great wave of antiradical and anti-immigrant feeling. Employers fired suspected radicals and mobs attacked known anarchists. Emma Goldman and others were arrested and abused before they could prove they were innocent of McKinley's death. The laws on immigration were tightened against anarchists, who were labeled "human garbage."

Chapter 7

The Troubles in Ireland

For prolonged and relentless political terror perhaps nothing compares with the Reconstruction period in America better than the stark reality of Northern Ireland today.

In just a few months of 1982 *The New York Times* carried reports of these terrorist actions, datelined Belfast or Londonderry:

February 2—IRA Provos seize and blow up British cargo ship.

March 3—IRA tries to assassinate Lord Lowry, Chief Justice of Northern Ireland; wounds professor greeting him.

March 6—IRA explodes car bomb, killing a nine-year-old child and injuring ten others. Four other bomb blasts reported in Northern Ireland within hours of one another.

March 26—IRA kills three British soldiers from ambush on Belfast street.

March 29—IRA gunmen kill inspector in Royal Ulster Constabulary as he leaves church service. "In the past 13 years, 54 reservists and 109 full-time members of the constabulary have been killed."

April 2—IRA shoots dead two British soldiers in civilian clothes riding in an unmarked van. "The deaths brought to 350 the number of British troops slain in 13 years of strife. The overall death toll is 2,185."

April 11—Bombs explode in three banks and two stores in Londonderry just before midnight, causing damage but no injuries.

April 18—Four gunmen wound farmer from ambush, then shoot him dead as he tries to crawl away from them. The killers apparently believe he was a part-time soldier, but he was not.

May 5—Gunman kills a police officer and wounds another seriously during a machine-gun attack on a patrol.

May 9—IRA gunmen wound five policemen in machine-gun ambush of two police patrols. In other violence the same day a fireman and a woman in downtown Londonderry are wounded when a bomb meant for security forces explodes, and a Catholic youth badly burns himself as he prepares to lob a gasoline bomb at a police patrol.

May 13—A Protestant and a Catholic are shot to death in separate attacks. Police theorize the Protestant was shot by the IRA and the Catholic by Protestant extremists.

June 26—The IRA detonates a 200-pound car bomb on a busy Belfast street outside a nurses' residence, wounding 24 nurses and one other person with flying glass and brick.

The newest phase of terror in Ireland began in 1969. But its roots go back eight centuries, to the day when Pope Adrian IV, the only English pope ever, gave control of Ireland to King Henry II of England. Four centuries later three revolts against British rule were crushed by Elizabeth I. In 1641 a ten-year rebellion began. With great cruelty Oliver Cromwell put down the rebels at a cost of 60,000 Irish lives. He settled more and more English—his former officers as well as militant Scottish Presbyterians—in Ireland, particularly in the North. In time Protestants owned a good part of the land in Catholic Ireland—land that had been taken by force from the Catholics.

The Irish nationalists see themselves as the people of Ireland. But they are not all the people of Ireland. They are the Catholic people of Ireland, a small minority of whom still speak the native Gaelic tongue. They were the losers in the Cromwellian wars and, having lost, suffered many forms of oppression—economic, social, cultural. Irish Catholics, in the eyes of the British Protestant Crown, were presumed to be disloyal. A presumption well founded, and naturally so. For more than 300 years the Irish Catholics have tried to get their own back, in a struggle that has both political and religious elements. The tactics used have shifted widely.

Over the years there were more uprisings against British rule, always followed by harsh repression. In the nineteenth century the goal of Irish nationalism was removal of barriers to ownership of land and discriminatory laws aimed at Catholics, improvement of conditions for Catholics, and Home Rule—an autonomous national status under the British Crown and Constitution. The people in favor of the reforms, the constitutional nationalists, had majority support. But there was a minority undercurrent of Irish republicanism, and its goal, in the words of its martyr, Wolfe Tone (a Protestant), was "to break the connection with England, the never-failing source of all our political evils."

The republican objective—a complete break with England—"could only be attained, if at all, by physical force," wrote Conor Cruise O'Brien, a present-day Irish statesman, "and Irish Republicanism was and is a physical-force movement."

Like other nationalist movements of Europe, the Irish Republicans formed into a secret, oath-taking society.

Founded in 1858, it fathered the Irish Republican Army (IRA) and its members became known as the Fenians (from Fianna—legendary Irish heroes). In 1867 a Fenian rising failed, and its leaders were condemned by the bishops for inciting people into a hopeless insurrection.

While most of the Irish supported the constitutional nationalists, they admired the Fenians for their courage and tenacity. The Fenians in theory stood for the unity of the Irish people of all denominations. But today's reality is something different. Their goal is breaking the connection with England, yet a million Irish people— the Protestants of Northern Ireland, comprising six counties in the province of Ulster—refuse to break that connection. They are unionists—in favor of keeping the union with England—and are determined to live as their ancestors have lived for centuries.

In the eyes of the republicans, the Protestant Irish are viewed as British—part of the occupying forces— or as traitors to Ireland. And "in either case," says O'Brien, "Republicans have warrant from their ideology to shoot these people down, whenever opportunity offers."

The overwhelming majority in Ireland in the early part of the century was in favor of achieving Home Rule by parliamentary action. The calls of the Fenians for violent revolt appealed to only a tiny minority. In 1914 a Home Rule Bill was finally approved by Parliament. But the Irish Protestants formed the Ulster Volunteers, staged mass demonstrations, and began arming and drilling to show their rock-hard refusal to be swallowed up in a Home Rule state with a Catholic majority. Faced with a choice of no Home Rule at all or an Irish Free State without six of the nine Northern counties of Ulster that together had a Protestant majority, the constitutional nationalists reluctantly agreed to the partition of Ireland. The Home Rule bill was shelved, however, upon the outbreak of the First World War. This was the time, the Irish Republican Brotherhood decided, to launch an insurrection. In 1916 came the Easter Rising in Dublin, crushed within a week. Only fanatical nationalists could have attempted such a reckless revolt with a handful of men against the whole British garrison and the police. The rising was not popular among Catholics when it was happening, and there was no mass uprising behind the rebels. But the execution of the leaders made a new roll of Irish martyrs, producing a deep revulsion against the British and a swing of public opinion to the republicans. Their political movement, called the Sinn Fein (Gaelic for "Ourselves Alone"), won a great election victory in 1918.

The new Irish Parliament proclaimed independence and set up a government of Ireland. That brought it into a state of war with Britain. But not all the Irish were united in the war. Many did not share the romanticism of the Easter Rising leaders and the cultural nationalists. Some still believed that a constitutional settlement with Britain could be negotiated. A small Protestant minority sided with the militant unionists in the North. And many Irish, Catholics and Protestants, dreaded a grim struggle for national independence that would also be a civil war.

For three years the IRA waged a guerrilla war against the Royal Irish Constabulary and British army units. The main tactics were raids on arsenals, police stations, military posts, and barracks, and the ambushing of larger and better-armed British forces. To break the British security system, Michael Collins (1890–1922), the IRA's chief strategist, developed a policy of selective terror. He did not want to use general terror against civilians because it would cost him public support. So he confined assassinations to intelligence officers and top police officials. (Of sixteen special intelligence officers sent to Dublin to track Collins down, thirteen were murdered.) The IRA also used terror against suspected informers, but avoided indiscriminate killings. Collins was a realist. He knew the IRA was never as strong as the British thought it to be, that it was short of weapons and could not survive an all-out assault the British were threatening to launch. He was ready to settle for a treaty even if it would not satisfy all the IRA's original demands.

The fighting ended in an Anglo-Irish Treaty in 1921. The treaty gave dominion status to the homogeneously Catholic southern part of Ireland, to be called the Irish Free State, but left the northern Protestant part (with some Catholic areas attached) still within the United Kingdom. The Irish (Catholic) people voted their approval of the treaty.

A minority of republicans, however, opposed the treaty—opposed it by arms. It isn't easy to stop guerrilla fighting or terrorism. For many it becomes a way of life. Some of the IRA couldn't see why the demand for an entirely independent and completely united Irish Republic couldn't be realized. They refused to give up the struggle. Outlaw gunmen they became, excommunicated by the Catholic Church. Many had come out of the ranks of the unemployed or from the small farmer class. Some had entered the IRA as teenagers and had never known any other life. It was hard to think of returning to humdrum civilian existence. But finally they were put down by the military power of the protreaty forces.

Today's IRA, too, insists that the Republic—because it is not *all* Ireland—is not the Republic the martyrs of 1916 died for. They claim that with Northern Ireland's continuing connection to Britain, Ireland is still not free. And they assert the right to use violence to achieve that goal of one Ireland.

In 1949 the Free State became the Republic of Ireland, the North remaining within the United Kingdom. But more and more militants over the next twenty years kept demanding that Ulster be united with the Republic. Although the Republic had outlawed it, the IRA prepared for action.

The Catholics in Northern Ireland had all along suffered from social, economic, and political discrimination. Unemployment in the Catholic districts was higher than in the Protestant. Local government, Protestant dominated, provided housing not on the basis of real need, but to their own political supporters, and when these were taken care of, they tended to forget about the Catholics and left them in intolerable slums. Political precincts and wards in certain areas were drawn unfairly, to Protestant advantage. This gerrymandering left Catholic voters with less representation than they were entitled to. In 1968 a civil rights movement was born, campaigning on such slogans as "One man, one vote," "Jobs on merit, houses on need," and "End gerrymandering." The movement used nonviolent demonstrations, petitions, and political pressure to gain civil rights.

Seeking a middle ground, the movement's leaders chose young Bernadette Devlin to run for a seat in the British Parliament vacated by death. She was a unity candidate for whom both republican and moderate Catholics could vote, and she won. Her victory was considered a major triumph for the civil rights movement. Devlin had been an unknown student of psychology at Queens University and now, at 21, she was the youngest woman member of Parliament ever, a young woman whose youth and gift of phrase gained her international attention. She had a very human way of voicing the feelings and thoughts of a great many people.

But blind to the real grievances of the Catholics, the unionists called the civil rights movement a front for an IRA conspiracy to make a revolution. The Reverend Ian Paisley, virulently anti-Catholic member of Parliament, whipped up a hate campaign that led to gang attacks and arson in the slums of Belfast, the capital of

Ulster. Street fighting broke out, terror on one side and then counterterror on the other. If the Protestant majority had granted the Catholic minority the rights they demanded, the terror might not have happened, or it might have been less bloody and costly.

As the sixties ended, the IRA split into two factions, both with leftist programs for Ireland's future. The larger wing, known as the Officials, seemed to be for a peaceful political course, forming alliances with other left groups and unions. The other wing, the Provisionals—Provos for short—felt only terror would unite Ireland.

Protestant mob violence brought British troops into Ulster in 1969. They soon were trying to stop the terrorists of both sides, for the Protestants had their version of the IRA, called the Ulster Defense Association (UDA). The Provos believed their terrorism would force the London government to withdraw the troops. But the British troops remain in Ulster, and the fighting between IRA and UDA has gone on ever since, with great losses on all sides.

Because of those losses, both sides began to recruit teenagers and even younger boys and girls. New generations of gunmen were bred. "Young people in both parts of Ireland," wrote Conor Cruise O'Brien, "have been brought up to think of democracy as part of everyday humdrum existence, but of recourse to violence as something existing on a superior plane, not merely glorious but even sacred." In just one year of the seventies, thirteen young boys belonging to the Provo youth division were killed.

A bus smolders in Northern Ireland after bombing by young
demonstrators. Both Protestant and Catholic groups engage
in terrorism in the hope of achieving their opposing goals.

More civilians than soldiers have been killed by the terrorists. From time to time the Officials and the Provos have even murdered one another. Terrorism in Ireland has been indiscriminate. Bars, stores, hotels, dance halls, clubs, movie houses, buses, trains, are favored targets for bombings. On both sides the terrorists have shown a cruelty, a viciousness, that seems almost crazed. It is worse than in the earlier days. Forty years ago when an IRA bomb plot went wrong, and killed five innocent people, the terrorists were horrified. They once tried to follow some kind of code of honor. No more. Now random bombs and bullets kill or cripple innocent Protestants and Catholics alike.

To carry out such murder, it always helps to assert the victims deserve it. Just as the Ku Klux Klan justified its brutal treatment of Blacks on the ground they were racially inferior, scarcely human, so did Protestant papers in Northern Ireland often describe Catholics as "slimy excrement," "two-legged rats," "Fenian scum" who must be exterminated. UDA gangs have resorted to the Klan's kind of terror and abuse in order to degrade and humiliate Catholics.

The hatred has grown so intense that some parents on both sides infect their children with it. From birth Ulster's babies are split by the sectarian passions, and the ugly fratricide lives on into the next generation. Boys and girls come to take a perverse pleasure in the tragic events, cheering their side on, jeering the other side, less and less sensitive to the pain and horror of human suffering. Fear and hatred poison the soul.

Where do the weapons of the terrorists come from? It is claimed that at one time perhaps eighty percent of the IRA's came from the United States. Most of the guns and explosives were paid for by donations of Irish Americans. Many of the donors didn't know, or said they didn't know, that their money bought weapons. (Publicly it was said to be for medical supplies and milk, or aid to families of imprisoned IRA members.)

Early in 1982 U.S. immigration officials broke up an IRA ring that crossed from Canada into the U.S. to buy weapons. Their "shopping list," a captured document revealed, included 200,000 rounds of ammunition that would fit machine guns, rifles, and pistols turned out by American, British, Czechoslovak, and Soviet arsenals. Also sought were electronic devices that could detonate bombs by remote control and small remote-controlled aircraft capable of carrying twenty pounds of explosives as far as five miles.

Some of the fund raising in recent years has been done in Ireland itself. And often by illegal means— bank robberies, protection rackets, drug dealing. In Ireland, as in many other places, terrorism can sink to the level of crimes that end in self-destruction. Aid for the Provos also came in from many other parts of the world, from nations and organizations supporting international terrorism.

The guns and bombs have splattered blood everywhere. In the last dozen years it is estimated the terrorists have cost Ireland 2,500 dead and 23,000 injured.

Some 900 others have had their kneecaps smashed for quitting or informing.

The price of terror, beyond the loss in lives, must include the shattering of community spirit, the division of families, the blunting of children's minds and feelings. How can business and industry be conducted normally under such conditions? Large sections of Belfast have been turned into heaps of rubble. The compromise essential to democratic politics is made impossible by cries of "treachery" and "betrayal." The ordinary citizen lives in a nightmare world where he cannot escape the terror of either side. Suspicion and hatred pollute the air everyone breathes.

Observers believe terrorism lacks support in both parts of Ireland. They see the tactic of planting bombs anywhere and everywhere as a sign of great political weakness, and as a despicable violation of human rights. But it might provoke the English to withdraw from Ulster, say terrorism's defenders. And if it does? Would everyone live in peace . . . or would the result be a terrible rise in bloodshed? And open civil war between Irish Catholics and Protestants?

At bottom Ireland's troubles are political. Yet both sides are seeking a military solution. More lives will inevitably be lost so long as that course is followed. Until the political necessities are dealt with, there will never be peace, only more murder.

The terrorists in Ireland would sacrifice lives for power—power for themselves or their cause. Theirs is a despotic drive no different from that of any other despot who determines to have his way regardless of how the majority think or what they want.

An Irish voice against terrorism was raised in debate in Dublin between Conor Cruise O'Brien and Thomas Mac Giolla, president of Sinn Fein (the Official IRA). O'Brien made these points about terrorism:

> I speak here for a Party which accepts normal democratic process. That acceptance includes recognition of the legitimate authority of an elected government which one does not like, and which one seeks to replace by democratic process. . . .
>
> Under democracy, civilians, not soldiers, have supreme power. And literally all sorts of people join in the choice of those civilians. The man who likes greyhound racing and reads the *Daily Mirror* has the same vote as a dedicated patriot who reads the *United Irishman*.
>
> People who value peace above national unification have votes. The military elite [IRA] for which Mr. Mac Giolla speaks decides that their votes don't count. For us, who accept democracy, all the votes count. . . .
>
> Now this division between those who accept democracy and those who don't accept it, is fundamental. If people disagree about that, their verbal agreement on other political matters is utterly deceptive. . . .
>
> If you set out to bring the society you want into existence through denying the validity of democratic process in the society you actually have; if you set out to win it through a private army, withdrawn from demo-

cratic control; if you set out to win it by exploiting the latent forces of romantic nationalism and hatred of foreigners, and if you hope to control these forces by authoritarian methods in your republic within a republic— if you set out in this way, then I say to you that the forces you hope to use and control will use and control you. . . .

Once you reject democratic process, and set the example of the private army, there is nothing to prevent any determined group, which can get its hands on guns and bombs, from setting up as the true heirs of the national tradition.

Chapter 8

An Eye for an Eye

The motive force for many terrorist groups, now and in the past, has been nationalism. By the end of the First World War the basic principle of the right to national self-government was universally accepted. The desire for the unity and self-determination of a people became a supreme value.

The power of the nationalist idea, the messianic fervor with which people believe in it, has often been deliberately used by parties and politicians for their own ends. The persisting terrorism of both the IRA and the UDA in Ireland cannot be understood without taking nationalism into account. And so, too, in the Middle East, where both Arab and Jewish terrorism were born out of nationalism.

Jewish Palestine was peopled by pioneers who came

to build new lives for themselves in a dream of Jewish independence and dignity. Palestine—the area including modern Israel, Jordan, and Lebanon—was under the Ottoman Turks in the nineteenth century; the Ottomans opened it to European settlement. Moses Hess (1812–72), a founding father of Zionism, put forth the view that the Jews were not held together by only religious bonds. They constituted a nation like any other. And in order to attain a full sense of their identity, they needed a state of their own. Hess, one of the first German socialists, rejected the European anti-Semitism that condemned the Jews to inferior status. He claimed no superior rights or powers for Jews. But he felt that without their own soil on the banks of the Jordan, the Jews could not fulfill their national life. In 1862 he published his *Rome and Jerusalem*, the first book to propose the idea that would be named Zionism thirty years later.

The Jews came into Palestine in successive waves of immigration. The first took place in 1881, when the assassination of Tsar Alexander II gave the excuse for scores of pogroms in Russia. The next wave came in 1904, then another at the end of the First World War, during which Palestine came under British control, and again in the mid-1920s. And then in the early 1930s, when the rise of Hitler menaced the Jews of Europe.

Those waves of immigration expressed the conviction of Theodor Herzl and the Zionist movement he organized in 1897. Jewish persecution stemmed from Jewish homelessness, the Zionists held, and the solution must be a "publicly assured, legally secured home" in Palestine, the ancestral home of the Jews. It was Chaim Weizmann and his political co-workers who secured from Great Britain in 1917 the Balfour Declaration. It pledged Britain would facilitate the establishment of a Jewish National Home in Palestine.

The Zionists knew, of course, that the British had made promises to the Arabs, too. But the Allied victory in the First World War had handed the Arabs sovereignty over 99 percent of the Mideast. New, independent Arab states of Saudi Arabia, Iraq, Syria, Lebanon, and Transjordan had been created. The common understanding was that the remaining 1 percent of that vast area would be set aside for the Jews.

Speaking for the Zionists was their organization, the Jewish Agency. Its aim was to cooperate with the British in achieving the goal of a Jewish National Home. As in any democratic organization, there were different views on how best to gain the common goal. The largest group was headed by Weizmann and David Ben-Gurion, leader of the Labor Mapam party in Palestine. They believed in gradually building up the country through constant immigration and settlement. The pioneers from eastern and central Europe would turn desert and swamp into farm and garden, creating a new society out of their own labor. Funds contributed by Jews worldwide would buy land in Palestine for the immigrants to settle. In the end a Jewish majority would develop, and they would then establish a Jewish state.

While most Zionists supported this approach, it was attacked by Vladimir Jabotinsky. A Russian Jew and a fervent orator, he did not believe in gradualism. The time for an independent Jewish state was now, he proclaimed. And it must be a state extending to the ancient and historic boundaries of Israel. He preached military preparedness. "It is necessary to plant and sow," he said, "but it is also necessary to shoot." The British might help, yes, but Jewish independence would be realized only by force of Jewish arms.

Jabotinsky was not just speculating about what might happen. There was ample evidence already that the Arabs in Palestine would not accept Jewish immigration peaceably. There were anti-Jewish riots in 1921, around the time Jabotinsky formed his Revisionist Zionist party to carry out his program. A new outbreak of Arab terror came in 1929. Then, for three years—from 1936 until the beginning of World War II—Arabs terrorized the Jews, attacking their settlements, destroying their farms, raping, looting, murdering. Their leader was the Mufti of Jerusalem. He had seized power over the Palestinian Arabs, encouraged by the successes of Hitler in central Europe and Mussolini in Abyssinia. A strike was organized against Jewish immigration, and in six months it turned into a guerrilla war against the Jews.

The British administrators of Palestine failed to check the violence of the Arab extremists. Instead they sought to appease the Arabs. It became dangerous for Jews to venture outside their quarters or to travel in the country without armed guard. In Arab shops and cafés Hitler's picture appeared next to the Mufti's. Swastika flags were seen on the streets.

Jabotinsky knew the military life, for he had helped found the Jewish Legion that had fought with the British against the Turks in World War I. He built a military youth movement, complete with uniforms, flags, trumpets, salutes, and obedience to the leader. His emphasis on the military did not sit well with most Palestinian Jews. But what distressed them more was his insistence that terror be met with terror. The majority believed that to shed blood except in self-defense would destroy the moral legitimacy of Zionism. The way to combat violent opposition, they said, was to build still more farms, more villages, more towns.

In 1937 the bitter dispute split apart the Haganah (Defense), the military arm of the Jewish Agency that was the secret volunteer homeguard defending the Jews against Arab attacks. Jabotinsky's people left to form the Irgun Zvai Leumi, or National Military Organization. The Irgun would no longer accept the authority of the Jewish Agency. Now it would practice "an eye for an eye." The Irgun would be the self-declared heart of an army the coming Jewish state would need. Like nationalist groups in other countries, it began to build a military structure, enforce discipline, and gather arms.

That same year the Palestine issue reached a new and more deadly stage. A British Commission studying the Palestine problem concluded that with the Jewish drive for independence and the Arab determination to resist it, the only solution was partition. (It was the same decision the British made in Ireland.) That meant dividing Palestine between the two peoples. The Zionist reaction was deep anguish, but the World Zionist Congress accepted partition. The Arabs opposed it. What right had the British to give away part of their homeland? It became an irrepressible conflict between two national communities within the narrow bounds of one small country.

Early in 1939, after a series of Arab attacks on Jewish settlements, the Irgun launched its first counterterror. Its bombs exploded in half a dozen Arab towns, killing scores of innocent men, women, and children.

The Haganah denounced the reprisals, putting out leaflets quoting the Bible: "Thou shalt not kill." The Irgun turned to the same Bible for reply: "Thou shalt give life for life, eye for eye . . . burning for burning. . . ." The British tried and failed to bring together Arabs and Jews for a London peacemaking conference. The Arabs refused to sit down with Jews.

Political events led the British to decide it was better to appease the Arabs than to meet the Zionist demands. Hitler had just seized Czechoslovakia and Mussolini had taken Albania. In May 1939 the British issued a White Paper on Palestine. It barred further land purchases by Jews in 95 percent of Palestine, unless the Arabs approved. It barred further Jewish immigration into Palestine after a five-year period during which 75,000 people would be admitted. Then no more except with Arab approval. It meant that the Jews would become an ever-decreasing minority. The document proclaimed that in ten years Palestine would become an independent Arab state.

The effect of the White Paper was to cancel the promise of the Balfour Declaration.

The Jews were enraged. This was appeasement by the same government that had just handed Czechoslovakia to Hitler. How could the British bar immigration when Europe was full of Jews desperate to escape being put into Nazi concentration camps? When refugee ships were trying to reach the shores of Palestine? When no other government was willing to take victims of Nazi persecution? When an open door to Palestine meant life to countless thousands?

There were demonstrations throughout the world against the new British policy. But the White Paper was not withdrawn. Now the militancy of the Jewish extremists did not seem so wild. Hadn't violence paid off for the Arabs? The White Paper had rewarded terrorism, punished self-restraint. The result was to make the British administration in Palestine the target of the Jewish terrorists. Its radio studios in Palestine were bombed by the Irgun as Jews rioted in the streets of the major cities. The British quickly rounded up almost all the high command of the Irgun and put some to torture. The Irgun countered with large-scale terror against both British and Arabs. They blew up a movie theater in Jerusalem, attacked an Arab village, destroyed British installations and communications. By the time Hitler marched into Poland, beginning World War II and dooming eastern European Jewry, the entire leadership of the Irgun was behind British barbed wire.

The outbreak of the war changed the course of history in the Middle East. Now Britain was fighting the common enemy, Germany. But it was the British who had shut the doors of Palestine to the Jews, sentencing them to die in Hitler's Europe. Still, thousands would manage to evade the Nazis and enter the stream of underground immigration carried by hundreds of small ships trying to run the British blockade of the Palestinian coast.

Faced with this dilemma, the Jewish Agency and the Haganah decided to "fight the war as if there were no White Paper, and fight the White Paper as if there were no war." Only gradually did the British army accept Jewish volunteers from Palestine. It feared that guns given Haganah fighters might someday be used against the British. And even as they took Jewish soldiers, they increased their efforts to prevent Jewish refugees from reaching safety in Palestine. When refugees succeeded in landing on Palestinian soil, the British forced them back onto the boats. Aboard the *Patria* the refugees blew up the ship and themselves in despair; all the passengers on the *Salvatore* drowned when the ship sank at sea. Those are but two examples of the bitter fruit of British policy.

Within the Irgun a debate raged over what to do about the question of cooperation with the British now that war had begun. One group decided to call a truce with the British while they fought the Germans, and to resume the revolt at war's end. The other group, led by Avraham Stern, would not cooperate with the British. By refusing to save Jewish refugees, said Stern, the British were collaborating with the Nazis in the destruction of the Jews.

Stern, in his thirties when he led his tiny band out of the Irgun, was to make his name synonymous with the bomb and the gun. He was born in Poland in 1907 and had come to Palestine at the age of fifteen. At the Hebrew University he was an outstanding scholar. But he gave up his academic studies to enter the underground. He helped form the Irgun and became one of its commanders. In and out of British prisons, he developed an intense anti-British passion, ready to walk with Satan himself, he said, if it meant the freedom of his people. Gerold Frank, a historian of Stern's group, describes its leader:

> [Stern] was one of the most unlikely persons to be cast in the role he played. . . . He was thirty-five, slender, strikingly handsome, with jet black hair; his face, narrow and aquiline, the nose and brow forming one straight line, the eyes dark and brooding, might have come from an El Greco canvas. He had a soft voice and tremendous charm. He was an excellent poet; he spoke perfect Russian and Polish, he had read Homer in the original, he knew Italian well and his Hebrew was out of the ordinary. A stranger meeting him would never dream that he was a terrorist. He did not indulge in fiery speeches; he seemed invariably calm, almost preoccupied; his manners were exquisite. But those who knew him recognized that for all his gentleness, there was a decision in his

tone which cut through all opposing argument: that under the velvet, the man was steel.

Stern seemed the model of the revolutionary intellectual, impatient with moderation or delay. With his small band he entered on a path of revolutionary terrorism that would lead most of them to prison or early graves. They began with no allies, arms, money, or popular support. All they had was a readiness to sacrifice for some end they never clearly defined. They collected money from each other and from friends. When that proved to be too little, they robbed banks—British, Arab, and Jewish. When they explained the revolutionary purpose behind theft, extortion, kidnapping, and murder, few would believe them. Even the extremists within the Irgun began to think them insane, and worse—traitors, when they learned Stern was trying to form alliances with any enemy of Britain, including Hitler and Mussolini. Nothing came of such secret missions except the arrest of his agents when they returned to Palestine. None of his operations—arms thefts, holdups, gun battles in dark alleys, posters on walls—inspired others or moved the frightened to fight.

Increasingly his terrorism took the lives of Jewish victims too. When several of Stern's men were tortured by a captain in British Intelligence, Stern lured the officer to a Tel Aviv apartment through an anonymous tip that it was a Sternist hideout, boobytrapping the place so that anyone opening the door would be blown up. The officer, sensing something wrong, did not lead the raid himself but sent two Jewish policemen. When they were killed instantly, the Jewish community denounced Stern as a murderer of his own people. The search for him intensified. He crept around Tel Aviv, sleeping in a different place each night. His picture was posted on every wall. Early in 1942 he was trapped in a hideout and shot while trying to escape. With the help of the Jewish community, appalled by the Stern Gang's operations, all but about 25 of his followers were captured.

But two weeks after Stern's death an ancient steamer called the *Struma*, with 800 Rumanian Jewish refugees aboard, was denied permission to land by the British high commissioner in Palestine, and sent out to sea again. There it broke apart, and sank within minutes. But for one survivor, all on board drowned. The tragedy, coming on top of so many others, made still more Jews believe that survival could be had only at the price of using the bomb and the gun.

In November 1944 came the most notorious act of terrorism committed by what remained of the Stern Gang. It was the murder of Baron Walter Edward Lord Moyne, British minister of state in the Middle East. The Sternists chose Moyne for assassination for three reasons: One, he carried out the policy of the British government and had to pay for that with his life, both as a symbol of British rule in the Middle East and as a personality. Two, the man appointed to succeed him would think twice before doing the same thing. And three, the act would shock the world, giving the Sternists the chance to explain their motives to everyone.

Two young members—17 and 22—of the Stern Gang were chosen to be the assassins of Lord Moyne. (They had never met before the assignment brought them to Cairo.) Eliahu Bet Zouri, the older terrorist, was born in Tel Aviv. Eliahu Hakim was born in Beirut and brought to Haifa as a child. Single-minded to the point of fanaticism, their underground connection was not known even to their parents. Both Eliahus were raised in a Palestine torn with terrorism. Before they reached their teens, they were running errands for the Jewish underground and had learned to hate the British. Bet Zouri, like Stern himself, was a fine scholar and an excellent maker of bombs. Hakim came from a wealthy family but lived in near starvation, giving all he owned to the movement.

The training of terrorists like the two Eliahus was designed to blot out the natural revulsion against an act of murder. Could you kill a man in cold blood? Could you shove a knife into his body? Could you pull the trigger if the man stood before you? And if he fell wounded, could you then fire again? How was it possible deliberately to kill another human being?

The solution of the terrorists was to develop a split personality. One side would master the technique needed to execute the deed. The other side would be intellectual, ordering the doing of the deed. The first would carry out the command of the second like a machine. Pull the trigger and then automatically pull it again and again, at least three times, to insure destroying the target. If you fired but once and only wounded the man, your instinct might be to give the helpless man first aid. So you must finish him off at once. Logic ruled. Once the act was dictated, conditioned reflex carried it out. Do it! One! Two! Three!

Lord Moyne's official residence was in Cairo, where he lived in a villa on an island in the Nile. His office was in the British Embassy. A tall lean man of 64, a widower for five years, he had been appointed to his post ten months before. He could not know his death this day had been planned many months ago. The terrorists had studied his every move and worked out all details to guarantee success. On this hot Monday morning he went to his office, worked until 12:30, then entered his car to be driven home for lunch and a rest. As the limousine stopped before his residence, two figures jumped out of the shrubbery, leaped the fence, and raced to the car. Both held revolvers, and when they reached the back door of the car, one wrenched it open and fired three shots at Lord Moyne. At almost the same moment, the other boy, standing cover for his companion, was jumped by the chauffeur. The boy fired three times at him. The driver died at once. Moyne was rushed to a hospital for emergency surgery, but died that night. Both young men had raced away on bicycles leaning against the fence, but were caught within minutes of the attack. They offered no resistance.

The assassination stunned the world Jewish community. The Hebrew press called the murder an "abomination." Said *Haaretz*, the leading Jewish paper in

Palestine, "Since Zionism began, no more grievous blow has been struck at our cause." In Jerusalem Dr. Leo Kohn, political adviser to the Jewish Agency, told the press, "When I think how proud we have been that Zionists could come before the world with clean hands as a creative movement of the highest order, and when I think of what these boys have been led to do . . ."

On March 23, 1945, Eliahu Hakim and Eliahu Bet Zouri were executed by hanging. Each sang the Hatikvah, the Hebrew song of hope, as he waited for the trap to be sprung.

A year later the rival underground group, the Irgun, committed an act of terror with much greater loss of life. They blew up the King David Hotel in Jerusalem, killing 91 Britons, Arabs, and Jews. The planner of that deed was Menachem Begin; 32 years later he would become the Prime Minister of the State of Israel.

The bombing of the King David Hotel was the consequence of a major change in Irgun policy. It had kept its wartime truce, refusing to attack the British while they fought the Nazis. But in 1944 it seemed clear that the Germans would soon go down in defeat. And Begin, a thirty-year-old Polish lawyer who had just become the new commander of the Irgun, decided to end the truce. He proclaimed war against Great Britain:

> There is no longer any armistice between the Jewish people and the British administration of Eretz Israel which hands our brothers over to Hitler. Our people are at war with this regime—war to the end . . . we shall fight, every Jew in the Homeland will fight. The God of

> Israel, the Lord of Hosts, will aid us. There will be no
> retreat. Freedom—or death.

Begin had fled occupied Warsaw on foot. He was
arrested by Soviet police and put in concentration camps
for a year, released only when he agreed to join the
Free Polish Army. When his unit was sent to Transjordan for training, he crossed into Palestine as an illegal immigrant. He had escaped the Holocaust, but
behind him were his father, mother, brother, and two
sisters, murdered by the Nazis. Jabotinsky had been his
idol; now Palestine was his homeland.

As a survivor of the Holocaust, he hated the de-
fenselessness and the homelessness of his people, which
had led to their doom. And the British? "We had to
hate," he wrote later,

> all those who . . . barred the way of our people to phys-
> ical salvation . . . and ruthlessly withstood their at-
> tempts to regain their national honor and restore their
> self-respect. Was there hate in our actions, in our revolt
> against British rule in our country? . . . To such a ques-
> tion the sincere answer is "yes."

He believed his was a God-given mission to make
sure a Holocaust would never happen again. The Irgun
were his freedom fighters waging a "revolutionary war
of liberation," the kind of partisan war the European
resistance fighters had waged against the Nazi occupiers
of their lands. But was Begin's parallel of the Irgun with
those partisans a valid one? A historian of the Irgun,
Thurston Clarke, makes these points:

[Begin] ignored the fact that the European partisans had been applauded by the democracies, not just because they were allies, but also because of the nature of their enemy. They were employing terror against the century's greatest terrorists. But responsible world opinion had never equated the British regime in Palestine with the Nazi occupation of Europe. The British Mandate was sometimes repressive, undeniably undemocratic, and capable of being cruel and arbitrary, but it was not a regime of terror. During the Mandate's thirty years fewer than a dozen Jewish underground fighters had been executed. No Jewish villages were blown up or plowed under and most Jews convicted of political crimes under the harsh Defense Emergency Regulations were accorded "special treatment" by British judges and segregated in prison from common criminals and Arabs.

He ignored, too, that the European partisans had been supported by majorities within the populations of the countries they sought to liberate. The Irgun was not. In 1946, two-thirds of Palestine was Arab and it certainly did not support any "liberation" which would lead to a Jewish state. Democratic elections had proved that 95 percent of the Jewish third supported the Jewish Agency and Haganah. The Irgun was a minority within a minority.

Equally committed to terrorism, the Irgun and the Stern Gang sometimes varied in their tactics. The Stern goal was to kill British soldiers and special police, and important British officials. The Irgun used sabotage, mostly blowing up buildings used by the British. But in planning explosions in buildings you could not be sure that large numbers of innocent people would be warned or evacuated in time. And so it was when the Irgun decided to strike a blow at the most visible symbol of British authority in the Middle East, the King David Hotel, headquarters of the British.

For a time, after the murder of Lord Moyne, the Haganah agreed to cooperate with the British to put down the terrorists. Zionist leadership believed terrorism would endanger their postwar objectives. During the period between October 1944 and July 1945, hundreds of terrorists were arrested, jailed, exiled. The policy of cooperation with the British broke down, however, when the Zionist leadership concluded that negotiations were not going to attain their goals. The implication was that terrorism was acceptable now, as the only way to make the British give up the Palestine mandate. (Competing terrorists in the Middle East would make good use of that example; so would the terrorists of many other parts of the world.)

The Holocaust had wrecked the policy of restraint. Most Palestinian Jews had hated terrorism. Their vision of their homeland was to build it by peaceful, humane means. In the face of Arab terror they had abided by a defensive policy, *havlagah*, the Hebrew word for restraint. The duty of the Haganah was to halt attacks upon Jews with the least amount of force and bloodshed, not to retaliate with terror.

But with the war's end in 1945 many Palestinian Jews would no longer draw a line between offensive and defensive struggle. Nonresistance, they felt, had meant the death of millions of Jews. And what had the liberal humanists in the Christian world done to save Hitler's victims? So in August 1945, when Britain announced the White Paper would still hold for Palestine, activists in the Jewish Agency agreed to let the Haganah work with the Irgun and the Stern Gang in launching separate but coordinated attacks upon government installations.

Weizmann and the moderates fought against that decision, fearing violence would corrupt Zionism. Said Weizmann: "I hate political violence. I am uncompromisingly against it. It can only do us harm; it can never do us any good. . . . But I cannot help understanding the reason why these young men are driven to despair."

On June 29, 1946—Black Saturday—25,000 British troops conducted raids all over Palestine in a declaration of war against the Jewish "extremist" elements. They ransacked the Jewish Agency offices, looking for evidence of links between it and the terrorist groups; forced their way into 25 settlements in search of arms and terrorists; and arrested nearly 3,000 Jews. Their methods were brutal, much like the Nazi roundups, ending here too with Jews penned behind barbed wire in detention camps. The purpose was to intimidate the Jews and bring the violence to an end.

To the Jewish Agency leaders in Europe, Black Saturday signaled the time to end participation in violence. The Irgun and the Stern Gang would go their own way, but the Haganah must confine itself to helping the illegal immigrants enter Palestine.

It was too late to abort the plan to destroy the King

David Hotel. The alliance of terrorists had already approved the Irgun attack upon the British Administration housed in the southwest wing of the King David. The British had taken every conceivable measure to safeguard their headquarters. But the rest of the place continued to function as one of the great imperial hotels. In the midst of the sentries, the barbed-wire barricades, the alarm signals, the sirens, the troops, the police, cocktails were served, elegant ladies chatted, businessmen dined over their deals, spies traded information, and journalists swapped rumors.

At noon on July 22 an Irgun assault unit, dressed as the hotel's Sudanese waiters with red cummerbunds and fezzes, rolled seven milk churns full of dynamite and TNT through a rear kitchen entrance of the hotel and into the empty Regence Grill. In an hour the restaurant would begin serving lunch. Those bombs had been in the Irgun's hands for three days. A last-minute note had reached Begin from the Haganah—"You should hold for the time being the Jerusalem operation." But with no explanation as to why, and no final date, he decided to go ahead. He had arranged for a warning to be given by telephone as soon as his agents had set the fuses on the bombs inside the hotel. A thirty-minute warning would give the British 25 minutes to evacuate, if all went well. His reasons for a warning? To permit Jews and other civilians to avoid harm, and because the Haganah had insisted on a warning. His aim this time was not to kill as many Britons as possible, but to terrorize them. By destroying their supposedly impregnable headquarters, he hoped to force them to leave Palestine.

At 12:37 P.M. the TNT in the milk cans exploded. The pressure was so enormous it burst the hearts, lungs, and livers of the clerks working on the floors above. The blast had the force of a direct hit of a 500-kilogram aerial bomb. The pillars in the Regence Grill that supported the floors above, housing the British Secretariat, disintegrated. The outer walls collapsed. The roof shot into the air. A shock wave blasted those standing close to the hotel. The suction ripped clothing off, tore rings from fingers and watches from wrists. Windowpanes crashed from the buildings nearby, cars rolled over, trees were uprooted. The King David Hotel became a huge cannon, firing pieces of concrete into the air at speeds of 100 miles per hour. They smashed cars, dug craters in the streets, and shattered passengers going by in buses.

What happened to the people inside the King David? Thurston Clarke describes the effect of the explosion:

> In that split second after 12:37, thirteen of those who had been alive at 12:36 disappeared without a trace. The clothes, bracelets, cufflinks and wallets which might have identified them exploded into dust and smoke. Others were turned to charcoal, melted into chairs and desks or exploded into countless fragments. The face of a Jewish typist was ripped from her skull, blown out of a window, and smeared onto the pavement below. Miraculously it was recognizable, a two-foot-long distorted death mask topped with tufts of hair.

Searching for bodies in the wreckage of the King David Hotel in Jerusalem, site of British Headquarters in Palestine. The building was blown up in 1946 by the Irgun, a Jewish terrorist group. In the bomb blast 91 people died.

Those in the Secretariat who survived this first, frozen split second endured a moment during which they understood what had happened—a bomb—and what might happen next—death. Then they were slammed by a hurricane of hot air, dust, and flames; knocked down, thrown up, somersaulting, sprawling, rolling, spinning, and helpless; blinded and choked by clouds of smoke and plaster, blistered by heat and deafened by clanging girders and exploding walls.

Blocks of stones, tables and desks crushed heads and snapped necks. Coat racks became deadly arrows that flew across rooms, piercing chests. Filing cabinets pinned people to walls, suffocating them. Chandeliers and ceiling fans crashed to the floor, impaling and decapitating those underneath.

Did the Irgun send a bomb warning on the day of the attack? The British had received so many warnings that turned out to be hoaxes that often they disregarded them. Their military officials insisted they never got a warning on the King David. Begin insisted fair warning had been phoned in, but no order had been given to evacuate the hotel. In Thurston Clarke's exhaustive study of the tragedy, he reports that Adina Hay, an Irgun courier, phoned in a warning at 12:22, fifteen minutes before the bomb exploded. The hotel's switchboard operator immediately notified the assistant manager, but he dismissed the warning as another hoax, and said, "Forget it."

Warning or no warning, 91 died in that bomb blast:

28 British, 41 Arabs, 17 Jews. Forty-six were injured.

The next day the Irgun announced it was responsible for the bombing of "the central building of the British power of occupation in Palestine." The Jewish world condemned the explosion and mourned the loss of life. The Executive Committee of the Jewish Agency called it "a dastardly crime" perpetrated by "a gang of desperadoes" who shed "innocent blood." One Jewish newspaper in Palestine called the Irgun "an evil gang of fascists." Another said, "This tragedy is sabotage committed against us and the integrity of our struggle." A third, *Haaretz*, said in an editorial:

> We came to this country not only to save ourselves from anti-Semitism and persecution, but to build a new and better life, based on the principles of justice which have been Israel's great contribution to world civilization.
>
> Has it been decreed that we should be guilty of all the sins and crimes of our enemies before attaining a haven of peace, the striving toward which has been the main motive force of Zionism? And if these are birth pangs of the Messiah, was that ancient Sage not right who said, "Let the Messiah come but I do not wish to see him"? The purpose for which those who committed yesterday's crime and their associates are striving, so they tell us, is a Jewish State. Even if murder could get us a State—which is more than doubtful—would that State be really Jewish? What would such a State be worth if we had to blind ourselves to all the moral values of our Jewish tradition and break all the commandments in order to attain it? The best of the Yishuv stands with weakened

forces, facing a rising tide of criminal, insane bloodshed. In very truth, the price is too great.

The Irgun continued its war against the British, with ever more brutal attacks. It took hostages and executed them, blew up buildings without warning, tried to assassinate British officials. Its terrorism, according to some historians, may have speeded up Britain's departure from Palestine. But it did not cause it; a much deeper force achieved that. The enormous cost to Britain of World War II had drained her resources and robbed her of the will to maintain her empire. In 1947 the United Nations voted to partition Palestine into Jewish and Arab states, and Britain announced it would withdraw its armed forces by May 1948.

In the interim, terror mounted. The Palestinian Arabs, enraged by partition, attacked Jewish civilians and murdered hundreds. The Irgun retaliated with bombings and killings, climaxing its terrorism with an attack upon the Arab village of Dir Yassin in April 1948, killing 254 men, women and children.

Five weeks later the British withdrew and the Jews proclaimed the State of Israel. The new state was immediately invaded by the armies of neighboring Arab countries. That war ended in an Israeli victory. The armistice agreements left Israel in possession of about 8,000 square miles of Palestine—21 percent more land than allotted under the partition plan. But it was assumed these borders were not final, only tentative. They were to be adjusted in later peace talks. That they were not altered left delayed-action time bombs that exploded in another and another and another war.

The terrorists had hoped the next generation would not need to make their choice of violence. Menachem Begin entered the new Israeli parliament as leader of the Herut Party, whose core consisted of his followers in the disbanded Irgun. His party was as uncompromising in its demands as the Irgun had been before. It insisted that Israel must expand to its full "historical" borders on both sides of the Jordan River.

The dream of the terrorists was flawed. There have been many more wars in Israel and many more dead. The Arabs remain, still refusing to give up their claim to their homeland.

Chapter 9

International Network

Terrorism by the Palestinian Arabs did not begin with the birth of the state of Israel. As we have seen, it goes back more than sixty years to the 1920s. It has continued almost without letup since Israel's War of Independence in 1948. Arab militants have never accepted the reality of a Jewish state and continue to organize armed resistance against it.

A national consciousness among the Palestinian Arabs emerged only with the creation of a refugee problem. In the short period between the 1947 vote of the United Nations for partition of Palestine and the withdrawal of the British in 1948, some 300,000 Arabs became refugees. The Arab leadership departed first, followed by the peasants who feared being left in a political and cultural void. With Israel's War of Independence another 400,000 refugees fled into neighboring Arab states. It was in the refugee camps and the large Palestinian

Arab communities of Jordan and Lebanon that a sense
of national self began to develop. Hatred grew for the
Israelis, as did resentment of the Arab states who failed
to help the Palestinians, as the displaced Arabs are now
called. But nearly twenty years passed as the Palestinians waited for Arab armies to help them recover their
homeland.

In 1964 a summit meeting of Arab states authorized
the Palestinians "to carry out their role in liberating
their homeland and determining their destiny." Soon
after, an assembly of Palestinian Arabs created the Palestine Liberation Organization, PLO. Its purpose: "To
attain the objective of liquidating Israel," to put it in
their own blunt words. And for that goal it established
a Palestine Liberation Army. The Army recruited fighters from among Palestinians scattered throughout the
various Arab countries. Its funds were donated by Arab
governments or levied by a tax on the Palestinians themselves.

One of the radical Palestinian groups was al-Fatah
(Arab Liberation Movement), organized several years
before. Its leaders wanted direct military action to re-
gain the homeland. From bases in Syria, and with Syrian
weapons and training, the al-Fatah ambushed Israeli
military patrols and inflicted many casualties.

In 1967 the Arab governments began crying out for
the "total extinction of Israel for all time" and took
open steps toward the launching of a holy war. The
PLO joined in, proclaiming bloodthirsty slogans. When
the Six Day War began that June, Israel smashed the

aggressors. With the Arab boasts that Israel was facing national extinction, the Jews knew they were fighting once more for the literal survival of their families and their people.

When the swift war ended, Israel occupied the extensive territories it had conquered during those six days in Sinai, the West Bank of the Jordan River, both halves of divided Jerusalem, and the Golan Heights. A few years later the Israelis decided that the notion of an independent Palestinian state was not realistic because it would mean turmoil in the occupied areas. So the government set about "creating facts" in these areas. The "facts" were Jewish settlements in the occupied territories, and the confiscation of land. The Arab world was outraged and called the process illegal. Others pointed out that the Israelis were only doing what conquerors in other wars always did.

The Palestinian Arabs, through al-Fatah, had carried out border violence before the Six Day War. After the June disaster they regrouped to intensify the terrorism. Leadership now came from Yasir Arafat. He was a short, balding, heavy-set man then in his late thirties. His pictures always showed him with a stubble of beard, dark glasses, and the checkered kaffiyeh (headdress). Arafat was born in Cairo of Palestinian parents. While at the university there he organized students in a militant anti-Israel group. He got guerrilla training in Egypt, went to Syria, and helped create the al-Fatah movement.

Al-Fatah declared that Palestinians, no matter what

country they were in, must remain free to make their own decisions. They pledged not to interfere in the internal affairs of Arab states. And they committed themselves to revolutionary violence to restore their homeland.

But then came the Six Day War. It wrecked the Arab armies. The Palestinians could no longer rely on the Arab governments to win back their homeland. Arafat took a new look at the unique situation created by the war. Here were occupied territories with large Arab populations, and they were now under Israeli military control. What could the Palestinians do about it? Arafat saw only one answer. The Palestinian militants were a weak and small force: Against the Israeli enemy, the only tactic was to escalate the use of terrorism.

Arafat and his followers thought the Israeli occupation regime on the West Bank and in Gaza would prove vulnerable to terrorist operations. On the West Bank al-Fatah threw grenades at Israeli patrols and detonated bombs in town squares, marketplaces, and bus terminals. As Arabs took jobs in Israel, al-Fatah tried sabotage of the work projects. Dynamite and grenades exploded in towns and cities. In 1968 the worst such incident killed 11 and wounded 55 Israeli civilians in Jerusalem. Dramatic and deadly actions, but they failed their goal—to spark a war of "national liberation" in the occupied Arab territories. The Israelis countered the blows with reprisals, killing or capturing hundreds of Palestinian fighters. Sometimes the Israelis were brutal: they leveled all 800 houses in one West Bank village and dynamited the homes of other Arabs without holding hearings or trials, or offering compensation.

Fear of Israeli punishment held back the West Bankers, but so too did the hard knowledge that the combined Arab armies had failed to defeat Israel. If they couldn't do it, how could al-Fatah and the other small terrorist groups that had sprung up? One of the newest such groups was the Popular Front for the Liberation of Palestine. It was led by George Habash, a physician born in Palestine of Christian parents, and now an avowed Marxist. His PFLP shared his goal of freeing not only Palestine from Israel, but also the Arab people from their reactionary regimes. His group splintered shortly into still smaller groups, quarreling over political and personal issues. But all shared one aim: to sabotage any possible peace agreement between Israel and the Arab governments, and ultimately to wipe Israel off the face of the earth. In all their propaganda they exalted violence.

The terrorist groups all operated under the political umbrella of the PLO. They were all based outside Israel, in neighboring Arab states, though of course they had members and sympathizers inside Israel. For a brief time terrorism racked the Gaza Strip, where hundreds of thousands of refugees nursed a deep hatred of Israelis. But the Israelis ended that by moving the refugees to new camps.

After 1970 the PLO carried on three kinds of terrorist actions. It fired shells and rockets into Israeli settlements from beyond the border. It infiltrated Israel with small terrorist units that attacked Israeli transports or settlements, sometimes taking hostages. And it carried terrorism against Israeli officials and other citizens into other countries, often by hijacking planes.

Two things distinguish the PLO from most other terrorist groups. One is the heavy financial backing it has; the other is the large outside political support the PLO receives. The reason for both conditions is not the grievances the Palestinian Arabs have against Israel. True, their grievances are legitimate, and their claims to homes they have lost or the independence they desire are valid. But they are no more valid than the claims of many other nationalist movements. What has made the PLO situation unique is this: The whole Arab world, with its powerful influence stemming from its vital oil production, both funds the PLO and obtains political backing for it from among many nations, including the Soviet Union.

Two crucial facts influence diplomatic and military decisions made on all sides: The modern industrial world needs oil, and the Arab nations of the Mideast and North Africa hold sixty percent of the world's oil reserve.

The United States, of course, is concerned with oil supplies, and anxious to prevent Middle East sources from being cut off or falling under the control of Soviet power. So while the U.S. has been the chief supporter of Israel—in diplomacy as well as financial and military aid—it tries to maneuver in the Middle East so as not to endanger its connections to both sides.

Acts of violence within Israel and the occupied territories had failed to advance liberation. Habash argued that the PLO should strike at Israel outside the state's borders and even beyond the Middle East itself. More sensational methods of attack awakened the whole world to the existence of the Palestinian Arabs and their cry for a homeland. The new tactics devised by the PLO were soon visible in the world's headlines.

It was shortly after the Six Day War that the PLO began to export its terrorism. It started in 1968 with the first hijacking: an El Al (the national Israeli airline) plane flying from Rome to Tel Aviv. Then two Arabs attacked an Israeli plane preparing for takeoff at Athens. They fired their guns at the plane's windows, killing one passenger. That too was carried out by the PLO faction headed by George Habash. He told an interviewer, "We think that killing one Jew far from the field of battle is more effective than killing a hundred Jews on the field of battle, because it attracts more attention." An Athens-bound Israeli plane was forced to land in Algeria, where 22 Jewish passengers were held hostage for five weeks, gaining vast publicity for the PLO. In the next two years the PFLP hijacked twelve more planes. They landed the last four—three American and one West European—in Jordan or Cairo, blowing up three of them on the ground while worldwide TV audiences watched. In 1970 one of their bombs blew up a Swiss airliner in flight, killing all 47 passengers and crew.

These acts of violence signaled the central role of the

Triumphant members of a PLO faction stand atop the wreck-age of a British airliner they blew up on the ground after hijacking it in flight. Passengers had been released before the jet was blown up.

PLO in international terrorism. The PFLP especially succeeded in recruiting anti-Israel leftists, international adventurers, and convicted criminals to share in their terrorist attacks. In the decade of 1967–77 over ninety percent of all terrorist acts in Western Europe were committed by members of Palestinian groups or by other terrorists on their behalf.

Training camps for the Arab terrorists had been established in the refugee camps and in the Middle East states of Jordan, Lebanon, and Syria. The most spectacular massacre by the PLO took place at Lod airport in Israel in May 1972, using Japanese terrorists as the gunmen. They murdered 27 people. One of the PLO hit teams killed eleven of Israel's Olympic athletes in Munich a few months later, and in 1973 murdered two American diplomats and one Belgian in Khartoum. Later that year they attacked a Pan American plane at Rome, killing 35 passengers and injuring dozens more.

Those Japanese "Red Army" commandos were but one example of international cooperation among terrorists. When Leila Khaled tried to hijack an El Al plane en route from Amsterdam in 1970, she was helped by an American terrorist who lost his life in the action. Turkish terrorists kidnapped and killed the Israeli consul in Istanbul in 1971. In 1975 when terrorists invaded the Vienna conference of the Organization of Petroleum Exporting Countries (OPEC), the attack team included not only Arabs but Germans and Latin Americans. They killed three and seized 81 hostages, including eleven OPEC ministers. They collected a record-breaking ransom of perhaps $50 million.

The intricate threads tying together international terrorism in training, weaponry, and actions were uncovered in the case of the three Japanese Red Army terrorists. Their training in arms and explosives began in Japan and North Korea, and continued at a PLO center in Lebanon. They obtained their forged passports in West Germany; they were provided with weapons in Rome, where they boarded an Air France plane for Tel Aviv, where they disembarked for the PLO assignment of murder. (Most of the victims of their machine-gun slaughter were Puerto Rican pilgrims.)

In the terrorist training camps expert instructors from several nations gave advanced courses to trainees from all over the world. Young men and women from Iran, Turkey, Japan, the Philippines, Ethiopia, West Germany, Italy, Spain, Ireland, and many countries of Latin America studied the tactics, weaponry, and propaganda of terrorism. Collaborating with Arab terrorists, the death squads made up of these disciplined graduates have been responsible for a grim record. Between 1968 and 1981 they carried out some 300 acts of terror outside Israel in which more than 300 persons were killed and 540 wounded. Their operations ranged over fifty countries, with West Germany, France, Britain, and Italy bearing the brunt.

While the PLO carried terrorism abroad, it did not cease its violence inside Israel. Artillery shells and rockets were fired across the border at Israeli settlements.

For three years after the Six Day defeat, the PLO made Jordan its main base for attacks upon Israel. Tolerated by Jordan's King Hussein, Arafat's guerrillas raided across the Jordan River against the Israel rule on the West Bank.

But Hussein became alarmed and then outraged as the PLO created a state within his state. He felt his rule was threatened and his very life was in danger. In September of 1970 his troops—mainly Bedouins who hated the Palestinians—fought and massacred the guerrillas. Driven out of Jordan, the surviving PLO forces regrouped themselves in Syria and Lebanon.

For a dozen years, into 1982, Lebanon was the main base of operations for the PLO. And again, as in Jordan, the PLO created a state within the state. It forced the Lebanese government to let it set up military bases near the Lebanese border with Israel. And not the Lebanese government but the PLO took direct control of the 600,000 Palestinians living within the country.

Small units of the PLO slipped across the border to kill, blow up water pumps, set fire to crops. In 1974 a few terrorists crossed the border into Ma'alot, a new town of mostly North African immigrant Jews. They seized a school in which 100 children and four teachers were spending the night on a holiday hike. The terrorists demanded the release of 26 Arab prisoners in return for the hostages. The Israelis stormed the school and killed the three terrorists, but not before the Palestinians had killed 22 of the children and wounded more than sixty. A similar terrorist raid on Kiryat Shemona

Israeli soldiers rush the wounded out of the school at Ma'alot, which PLO terrorists seized, holding the children hostage, in 1974. The terrorists killed 22 of the children and wounded over 60 before Israeli troops stormed the school.

the month before had cost the lives of eighteen people, eight of them children.

The PLO policy of murder and sabotage continued into the 1980s. At least eight terrorist groups were now under the umbrella of the PLO. They had made Lebanon the world capital of international terrorism. That nation had been dismembered by Syria and the PLO in 1977. Syria had handed a chunk of occupied Lebanon to the PLO, which used it as a base for importing arms and exporting terrorism. Fighting across the border between Israel and the Palestinians in southern Lebanon had come under a cease-fire agreement in July 1981, arranged by the United States.

In June 1982 there was a large-scale Israeli invasion of Lebanon, ordered by the Israeli government (now headed by Menachem Begin) and led by Defense Minister Ariel Sharon. It was an operation, they said, aiming to stop the PLO shelling of the Galilee and secure a 25-mile safe zone north of the Israeli border. But the invasion did not end until the PLO forces were driven out of West Beirut, much more than 25 miles from the border. The Israeli defense forces displayed overwhelming power and skill. They uprooted the PLO from Beirut and south Lebanon, captured its arms caches, destroyed its military structure, and changed its political position in the Arab world.

The victory came at great cost to Israel, both within and outside the country. The intensive bombing of civilian residence areas in West Beirut and the September massacre, by Israel's Lebanese Christian allies, of hundreds of civilians in two Palestinian refugee camps were seriously damaging. The morality of the government's use of military power for political ends was fiercely debated within Israel and by friends of Israel in America and elsewhere. For the first time Israel was seen to be using its military strength much as a superpower does—that is, to shape the internal policies of another country.

With the ouster of the PLO from Beirut and south Lebanon came an opportunity to make progress on the Palestinian question. Three eminent Jewish leaders pointed a new direction during the Lebanese invasion. In a statement issued in Paris, Pierre Mendès-France, a former prime minister of France; Philip Klutznick, former chairman of the Conference of Presidents of Major American Jewish Organizations; and Nahum Goldmann, the president of the World Zionist Organization and of the World Jewish Congress, said this:

> Peace need not be made between friends, but between enemies who have struggled and suffered. Our sense of Jewish history and the moral imperatives of this moment require us to insist that the time is urgent for mutual recognition between Israel and the Palestinian people. There must be a stop to the sterile debate whereby the Arab world challenges the existence of Israel and Jews challenge the political legitimacy of the Palestinian right for independence. . . .
>
> The war in Lebanon must stop. . . . And there should be negotiations with the aim of achieving coexistence between the Israeli and Palestinian peoples based on self-determination.

If Israel continues to reject the reality of Palestinian aspirations, it takes on an enormous psychological, social, and economic burden. How can Israel absorb a huge Arab population on the West Bank and in Gaza without coming to resemble South Africa with its apartheid policy? Or without creating for itself another Northern Ireland?

And can the Palestinians continue forever their futile reliance on terrorism? For many decades the strategy of terror has failed to advance their cause. It has failed for them as it has failed in Argentina, Chile, Brazil, Uruguay, West Germany, Italy. . . . Lebanon proved how feeble Arab military power is. If the Palestinians do not give up their military fantasies, can they offer their people anything but one disastrous war after another?

No, dependence upon violence seems to have reached a bloody dead end. Extremists on both sides have proved that military solutions do not work. Surely sane people with moderate views and a belief in equal justice can find a way to negotiate a peace that will bring an end to generations of war in the Middle East.

Chapter 10

Mini-Manual for Terrorism

When their bomb blew up Tsar Alexander II, Sophia Perovskaya's band of terrorists expected that their deed would bring about revolutionary changes in Russia.

The result was only to make things worse.

But that was an act of individual assassination. How different have the results of systematic terrorist campaigns been? Terrorism that has struck repeatedly and relentlessly against many targets in a nation, year after year?

We could go to any quarter of the globe for examples of such systematic terrorism. What happened in Uruguay may provide the evidence to answer the question. For a long time—up to 1972—Uruguay was highly regarded as an advanced and stable democracy. But today Uruguay is one of the many nations in Latin America where a brutally repressive government is in power. In

1978 the Inter-American Commission on Human Rights issued a report charging the Uruguay regime with wholesale violations of human rights, including arbitrary arrest, torture, and murder of political prisoners. So many people were thrown into jail that on a per capita basis Uruguay could boast the largest concentration of political prisoners of any country in the world—one for every 450 citizens. The commission produced evidence that torture methods used by the Uruguay military and police included beatings of all types; electric prods for sensitive parts of the body; repeated immersions upside down in tanks of water mixed with vomit, blood, or urine; and sexual acts of violence.

What happened in Uruguay?

As far back as the early 1900s Uruguay had enjoyed a political democracy and a social welfare system that reached out to meet the needs of all. A small country wedged in between two giants, Brazil and Argentina, it now has about three million citizens. Over half of them live in Montevideo, the capital and the largest city. Uruguay long ago provided free public education up through the university, producing a literacy rate of over ninety percent, one of the world's highest.

In the mid-1950s the country began to run into economic trouble. Inflation and unemployment put great strain on the welfare system and caused widespread unrest. By the early 1960s it was felt something had to be done to solve the country's urgent problems. Many other Latin American countries were experiencing similar difficulties. And in several of them revolutionaries, mostly students from the middle class, concluded that talking wouldn't help much. The pace of change was too slow, the people suffering hardship weren't organizing in sufficient strength to change government policies in their favor.

In 1963 the Uruguayan students founded the Movimiento de Liberacion Nacional (MLN). Calling themselves the Tupamaros, they would soon become one of the best-known terror organizations on the continent. Their name came from an Inca prince, Tupac Amarú, who fought Spanish rule in the eighteenth century. He was executed in Lima, torn apart by four cart horses. His name, shortened to Tupamaro, came to mean troublemaker throughout Latin America. Two centuries later the small band of Uruguayans adopted it as a badge of honor.

The Tupamaros confronted a liberal government (unlike Brazilian terrorists, who faced an army dictatorship). Theirs was a society open to change by democratic means. Under liberal regimes the country had developed the best health care in Latin America, the lowest mortality rate, the oldest system of social insurance, and a strong trade union movement. But corruption had crept in, and the pace of reforms to meet the devastating economic problems was slow.

The Tupamaros had scarcely fifty members when they started. They tried to recruit among the working class, but did not get very far. Most of their members were drawn from students, teachers, and other professionals. Like middle-class rebels everywhere, they felt guilty about their own privileged position and driven to commit themselves to revolutionary change. There was a Communist party, but it was not militant enough for the Tupamaros.

At first the Tupamaros did not shed blood or destroy property. They saw themselves as Robin Hoods, robbing the rich to give to the poor. They hijacked trucks, held up banks and businesses and gambling casinos, and sometimes handed the swag to workers. And they raided arsenals to gather weapons.

Their leader was Raul Sendic, a law student and a Socialist. Fed up with the Socialist party, he tried to organize sugarcane workers but became disillusioned with unions too. He believed the economic structure of Uruguay had to be destroyed before the country's wealth could be distributed to wipe out poverty. But no killing, said the Tupamaros. Only in self-defense. Inevitably there was bloodshed when the police interfered with their kidnappings and robberies. Still, they insisted they tried to avoid harming innocent victims because that would turn the people against them. But if their main goal was to weaken the regime's support by provoking it into harsh repressive measures, how could they overlook the terrible harm that would be done to millions of innocents by those same repressive measures?

In the late 1960s the Tupamaros thought they had found the key to speeding up revolutionary change. If they could force the government into a deep crisis, then the old system could be overthrown. What could bring about such a crisis? Their answer: guerrilla warfare in

the cities. The radicals recognized that Latin America
had the fastest rate of urbanization in the world. The
majority of the populations lived in the cities. That's
where the power was—economic, political, military. So
they decided to attack that power in the cities.

They found a blueprint for urban warfare in a 48-
page book written by Carlos Marighella. For forty years
a leader of the Brazilian Communist party, he had left
in disgust because of what he saw as a slow and feeble
effort to reform government. Like many of the young
radicals who would follow him, he wanted revolution,
not reform, and he wanted it right away, not in some
dim future. He published his *Mini-Manual for Urban
Guerrilla Warfare* in 1969. Translated quickly into many
languages, it became the bible of terrorists around the
world.

Violent action was what the *Mini-Manual* called for,
and the more destructive, the better. Marighella's book
tells how to blow up bridges and railways, how to sabotage oil pipelines, how to destroy food supplies, how
to raise money by bank robbery and kidnapping for
ransom, how to kill army and police officers, how to
execute spies and informers. It spells out the terrorists'
need to master dozens of skills to carry out their missions, from flying planes and sailing boats to forging
documents and concocting deadly drugs. It specifies the
best weapons for particular jobs, stressing that "shooting and aiming are to the urban guerrilla what air and
water are to human beings."

The central idea behind the strategy of terrorism is

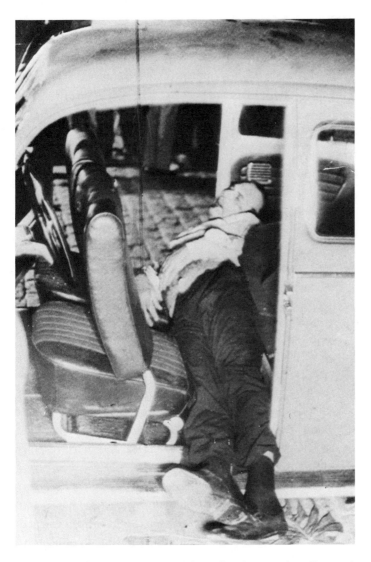

Carlos Marighella, Brazilian author of an internationally used *Mini-Manual* for terrorists, lies slumped across his car seat, shot to death in a police ambush.

an old and ugly belief: the worse, the better. Again and again political radicals operating in a democratic society have hoped for, or worked for, the use of repressive measures by the government so that the citizens will suffer enough to turn to the revolutionary movement for a way out. When Hitler's star began to rise in the Germany of the 1920s, the Communists, instead of uniting other anti-Nazi forces to stop Hitler, used to sloganize: "After Hitler, us!" Everyone knows the tragic outcome of that policy. Here is how Marighella, thinking like the German radicals, puts the case for his revolutionary violence:

> The government has no alternative except to intensify repression. The police roundups, house searches, arrests of innocent people, make life in the city unbearable. The general sentiment is that the government is unjust, incapable of solving problems, and resorts purely and simply to the physical liquidation of its opponents. The political situation is transformed into a military situation, in which the militarists appear more and more responsible for errors and violence.
>
> When pacifiers and right-wing opportunists see the militarists on the brink of the abyss, they join hands and beg the hangmen for elections and other trips designed to fool the masses. Rejecting the so-called "political solution," the urban guerrilla must become more aggressive and violent, resorting without letup to sabotage, terrorism, expropriations, assaults, kidnappings and executions, heightening the disastrous situation in which the government must act.

What did Marighella hope would come out of all this? The collapse of the government in power. Unable to control the widespread violence, it would give way to the terrorists.

Shooting—that was the most important thing. More important than any other activity, especially talking about ideas. Marighella and his followers sneered at ideology and traditional politics. The society of the future, they believed, would be built not by speech makers and resolution writers, but by those steeled in the armed struggle. Political details were trivial. Better not to worry about what the revolutionary future would be like. Arguments over that would only split your followers. Don't make specific political statements. Be vague about your aims. "Words divide us, actions unite us."

That vagueness was not simply a deliberate device to avoid scaring off people who might not agree with you. It was a sign too of how uncertain and confused the radicals were in their political thinking. It helps make clear why so many of them found it easy to switch from one political group to another, often leaping even from extreme right to extreme left or vice versa.

Uruguay offered the first example outside Brazil of what Marighella's brand of terrorism would do. He himself was already dead by the time the Uruguayans applied his blueprint. Soon after his *Mini-Manual* appeared, he was killed in a police ambush. His bloody prescription had done nothing to cure Brazil's ills. It had only made the sick patient worse. What failed to occur was the overthrow of the old system. Terror provoked his country's military into even more terrible repression, and the despots still rule that land.

But the Uruguayan students of the *Mini-Manual* saw no lesson in the outcome of its application in Brazil. In 1970 they switched from playing Robin Hood's merry men to murder. They were organized into secret groups, each with an assigned specialty or duty. Some were firing squads, some ran the "people's prisons" where the kidnapped were kept, others became the links to terrorist movements outside Uruguay. In the words of one reporter, they "bombed, burned, robbed, kidnapped and killed with a dazzling display of nerve, skill, discipline, inventiveness and bravado."

Their sensational exploits are typified by a raid they made against the town of Pando near Montevideo. Disguised as members of a funeral procession, about forty Tupamaros attacked the police station and telephone exchange, and robbed four banks of a quarter of a million dollars—all in fifteen minutes. During the raids they shot and killed policemen in street battles. That year they took as hostage Dan Mitrione, a U.S. adviser to the Uruguayan police force, who, they charged, was actually training the state security force in the techniques of torture. When the government refused to exchange political prisoners for Mitrione, they "executed"—murdered—him. And the next year they went on to kidnap a British diplomat, an American cultural adviser, and the British ambassador, Sir Geoffrey Jackson, confining Jackson in a cage six feet by two feet for the next eight months.

Murder followed murder as the police net tightened around them. In two years the Tupamaros carried out over 300 recorded assaults. They invaded and occupied airports, police stations, and broadcasting studios. They blew up homes, public buildings, automobiles, and shops. After the killing of Dan Mitrione they made victims of a former cabinet minister, high-ranking police officers, a naval captain, a prison chief. Sitting at the controls of the terrorism in the heart of Montevideo was Raul Sendic, now unrecognizable. He had been captured by the police, but had escaped and had his face completely remade by a plastic surgeon. Jailbreaks were easy because the guards were inefficient and corrupt. Sendic himself, with the bribed aid of the guards, led 106 Tupamaros to freedom through a tunnel leading out of a maximum security prison.

The terrorists intensified their violence early in 1972. They decided to launch a "direct and systematic attack against the repressive forces." It came at a strange time. A few months before, the Tupamaros and nonterrorist leftists had joined in support of a political coalition in a national election. But their candidates had won only twenty percent of the vote. It proved how cut off the terrorists were from the people they said they acted for. To engage now in big battles against the armed power of the state was either foolish bravado or the desperate, suicidal gesture of those who know they are doomed.

Proof was plain that the Tupamaros had gravely overestimated their support among the people of Uruguay. Now they would show how badly they underestimated the strength of the state's armed power. In hit-and-run battles against the army and police the terrorists killed many people. They set themselves up as judge, jury, and executioner. Their "people's courts" and "people's prisons" gave them the illusion they were already an "alternative power" to the real government. "The Tupamaros are the people and the people are the Tupamaros" was a ringing slogan, but how far from reality it was!

When the police proved unable to halt the mounting violence, the army took over the struggle against terrorism, using torture and its own brand of terrorism. It ended with the destruction of both the Tupamaro movement and Uruguay's civil liberties. A military junta seized power in 1973. It swiftly banned all political parties, unions, and student groups. It has ruled the country ever since.

What had the Tupamaros succeeded in doing? In his study of international terrorism, Walter Laqueur sums it up:

> [The Tupamaros] were genuine idealists; some of the best of the young generation belonged to them. Their activities were initially quite successful, proving that civilian governments could easily be disrupted and providing striking headlines for the world press. But in the final analysis, the only result of their campaign was the destruction of freedom in a country which, alone in Latin America, had had an unbroken democratic tradition of many decades and which had been the first Latin American welfare state.

True, the Uruguay of the 1960s was far from perfect and was faced with serious economic and social problems, but it is doubtful whether the Tupamaros had a better answer to these problems than the government of the day. The Tupamaros' campaign resulted in the emergence of a right-wing military dictatorship; in destroying the democratic system, they also destroyed their own movement. By the 1970s they and their sympathizers were reduced to bitter protests in exile against the crimes of a repressive regime which, but for their own action, would not have come into existence.

The gravediggers of liberal Uruguay also dug their own grave.

Chapter 11

To Light a Torch

It began when Andreas Baader and three other young people set fire to two department stores in Frankfurt in April 1968. In the fifteen years since then, many other acts of terrorism have been committed in West Germany. One terrorist group after another has risen to the headlines, then passed out of the news after arrests, trials, imprisonment, suicide.

The most notorious of them is known as the Baader-Meinhof gang. It was the first in West Germany to form a terrorist movement. Although many of its members were captured by the police—accused of murder, robbery, bombing, kidnapping, shooting, criminal conspiracy—and imprisoned after trial, the gang still carries on its underground warfare.

The group rose out of the student protest movement that swept the United States and Europe in the 1960s.

Toward the end of that decade public demonstrations died down. But the Vietnam War, the symbol to the young people of power used for evil ends, still went on. Some of the student activists had moved from pacifism through civil disobedience to violence. In May 1967 a terrible fire ravaged a department store in Brussels. A few days later a political pamphlet was circulating among students in Germany. It said the Belgian fire had been planned to create "warlike conditions" among the 4,000 shoppers and employees in the Brussels store. The pamphlet went on to describe the "superscale happening" in these terms:

> The store was one ocean of flames and smoke. Panic broke out among the people, many of whom were trampled underfoot. Some fell like burning torches from the windows. Others lost their heads and jumped into the street and were smashed to pieces. Eyewitnesses report, "It was a picture of the Apocalypse." Many, screaming for help, died of suffocation. Only after seven hours was the fire conflagration under control. The damage is estimated at $45 million.

Then came another pamphlet, headed "When Will the Berlin Stores Burn?" It said:

> Our Belgian friends have now discovered the trick of how to let the population take a real personal interest in the merry goings-on in Vietnam; they set fire to a store, three hundred satiated citizens and their exciting lives come to an end, and Brussels becomes Hanoi. Now no one needs to shed tears for the poor Vietnamese

people over his breakfast paper. As for today he can
simply walk into the made-to-measure department . . .
and discreetly light a cigaret in the dressing room. . . .
If there's a fire somewhere in the near future, if an army
barracks goes up into the air, if in some stadium a stand
collapses, be little surprised. . . .
Burn, warehouse, burn.

Those words voiced a frightening indifference to human
suffering. Those who set the fire were murdering the
shoppers and workers in the store for their presumed
indifference to the war in Vietnam. At the same time
the arsonists were condemning people for shopping to
satisfy their material needs. Mostly members of the
middle and upper classes who could afford anything
they wanted, the terrorists seemed to envy the suffering
of the world's poor. Committing arson in German department stores would be their sadistic way of bringing
the Vietnam War home to a consumer-sick society.

Less than a year later, Andreas Baader's gang would
deliberately burn the Frankfurt stores by means of fire
bombs. Baader, 25 when he began his terrorist career,
was the son of a German soldier who died on the Russian front. The young Andreas was remembered by his
schoolmates as a sulky bully who hated to study or
work. At twenty he went to Berlin and began to live
off the several women who found him attractive. In
1967 he met Gudrun Ensslin. She was the daughter of
a pastor whose church opposed blind obedience to authority. Through her family Ensslin developed a deep
concern for social justice and a hatred of war. At the

university she met Bernward Vesper and joined him in editing a literary magazine. They campaigned for socialist candidates but became disgusted with their party when it made an alliance with conservatives. They lived together and had a child, whom they carried to political rallies. When a student was shot by a policeman during a demonstration against the visiting Shah of Iran, Ensslin's reaction was to blame the death on "the generation of Auschwitz." By that she meant the older generation, who had shared in the crimes of Hitler's Germany. She called for the students to arm themselves. No longer a pacifist, she became the leader of those who wanted to fight it out with the government on the streets. They spoke of themselves as the Tupamaros of West Germany. The system was the enemy and the radicals must work outside it. "Violence to meet violence!" Ensslin preached.

In less than a year after her son's birth, Ensslin called motherhood a trap and left her baby, his father, and her home to live with Andreas Baader. They moved to Frankfurt, where the university radicals they linked up with would beat up students they disagreed with and wreck the offices of professors they disliked. Gudrun called constantly for action and more action. And shortly she and Andreas, with two others, firebombed the department stores.

An informer denounced them to the police. Brought to trial seven months later, they showed no signs of guilt. They claimed a high moral purpose: "To light a torch for Vietnam." They refused to defend themselves in a court that was merely an instrument of the capitalist system. They were found guilty of arson endangering human life and given three years in prison.

The response of the students to their crime was varied. Some disapproved it, while others, excited by its daring, applauded. In their minds it was a lofty deed of great historical importance.

One of those who approved it was Ulrike Meinhof. Her parents, both art historians, had died when she was young, and she was raised by a foster mother who was a professor of education and a deeply religious woman. At college Meinhof was drawn into the campaign against atomic weapons. She fell in love with a left-wing student editor, Klaus Rainer Rohl, who convinced her that "the mighty dream—justice—would be realized solely through communism." Meinhof began writing a popular column about social problems for Rohl's paper, *Konkret*, which was at first secretly financed by East Germany.

She married Rohl and moved further to the left, joining the illegal Communist party and working with her husband on his magazine. It hit a crisis when the East Germans withdrew their backing. To save *Konkret*, Rohl turned it into a porn-with-politics magazine, boosting the circulation enormously. Meinhof's column put her on TV talk shows as the champion of the underdog. She became a great success as one of the few women journalists, and the now-prosperous Rohls entered fashionable society. Meinhof's radical fervor amused the rich, who petted the subversive in their midst.

But the example of the Frankfurt arsonists made her

uneasy about her own soft life. She was writing about the problems of neglected children, and about the exploitation of foreign workers in German factories, while she herself enjoyed comfort and security. This contrast began "to tear her to pieces," she said. The next year she left her husband and, with her two children, moved to Berlin. When the Russians invaded Czechoslovakia in 1968, she lost faith in Soviet communism.

Now despairing of political parties, she was ready to act on her own to make the world what she wanted it to be. While she worked for *Konkret*, she had been sent to cover the trial of the arsonists and interviewed Baader and Ensslin. While "arson cannot be recommended," she wrote, "still it is better to burn a department store than run one." She seemed to be listening for a signal to violence.

Released from jail pending appeal, Baader was caught violating parole. Meinhof visited him in jail and confided she was willing to help him escape. He got permission to spend a day, under guard, at a research institute to collect material for a book he and Meinhof were supposedly to write. There Meinhof and a few others engineered his escape. During the shoot-out an institute worker was seriously wounded.

The rescue of Baader by Meinhof marked the birth of the terrorist gang that would bear their names. They took as their model the Tupamaros of Uruguay, now at their sensational peak. From the underground Meinhof wrote a handbook on urban guerrilla warfare while the search for her and Baader went on. The real strategist of the gang was Horst Mahler, a young radical lawyer who had defended Baader in the Frankfurt arson trial. He was credited with writing a manifesto that called for armed struggle by commando groups and gave instructions on making weapons. "Violence," it said, "is the highest form of class struggle."

A few weeks after Baader's escape he and Meinhof and Gudrun Ensslin reached Jordan on false passports. There they entered a PLO camp for training as urban guerrillas. But they did not get along on personal grounds with the Arab terrorists, and after two months returned to Germany to launch their "People's War."

It takes money to finance a war. They found the way to do it in Carlos Marighella's *Mini-Manual*. "Do it yourself," he advised. Robbing banks is the best way to start. You get capitalism to finance its own over-throw. Mahler divided the gang into four groups. They broke into four banks on the same day at the same hour. It was a promising beginning, except that a tip to the police soon led to the capture of Mahler and three others.

So it went for the next two years. The gang robbed more banks, bombed U.S. Army headquarters in Germany, bombed corporation buildings, bombed police headquarters, bombed judicial offices, bombed newspaper offices, bombed cars. Many victims were mutilated, several were killed. By the end of May 1972 most of the left in Germany had had enough of the Baader-Meinhof gang. It had done nothing but harm to the cause. The whole country was in danger of swinging sharply to the right in revulsion against these outrages.

Finally, in June 1972, the leaders of the gang were all caught: Baader, Meinhof, Ensslin, and two others. Three years later four of them, including Baader and Meinhof, were brought to trial; the fifth died from the effects of a hunger strike before trial. The main charges against the gang members were the murder by means of time bombs of four U.S. soldiers, the attempted murder of 54 other persons, robbery, and the forming of a criminal group. One of the state's key witnesses was a former gang member who told who had set the bombs, where, and how.

Toward the end of the long trial, Gudrun Ensslin confessed to three of the deadly bombings with which they were charged. A few days later, when a guard opened Ulrike Meinhof's cell in the morning, she found the prisoner hanging from the crossbar of her window. Apparently, Meinhof had made a rope by tearing her towel into strips. She had stood on a chair, tied the rope to the crossbar, put the noose around her neck, and jumped. She had been dead for some hours when her corpse was discovered. Specialists appointed by the state and others appointed by the defense agreed with the official finding of death by suicide.

Many in the left charged that Meinhof was murdered by the state. Jillian Becker, in her detailed study of the gang, concluded that the evidence was all against that. She added:

> But those who desired to make a martyr of Meinhof would not be deterred by evidence anyway. And if those

Ulrike Meinhof, a leader of the Baader-Meinhof terrorist group in West Germany, is taken into custody by the police. She died in prison.

who started these rumors of violent assault and murder were themselves sympathetic to the urban guerrilla movement, they could be expected to deny that Meinhof committed suicide or was a suicidal type. The [gang] and its sympathizers pretended that the members of the group acted for political motives only, never out of private emotion. A suicide was a denial of that lie; it challenged the pretense that they were sterilized of all feelings except the fervor for revolution.

With the nucleus imprisoned or dead, a new leadership took over the Baader-Meinhof Gang. The Heidelberg lawyer Siegfried Haag switched from giving legal counsel to the gang to running it himself. Training of recruits continued in the Middle Eastern camps run by the PLO. One of the first terrorist actions directed by Haag was the seizure of the German embassy in Stockholm in 1975. The terrorists demanded the freeing of 26 Baader-Meinhof prisoners, with $20,000 apiece and an airliner to fly them away. The raiders killed two hostages and mined the upper floor of the embassy with dynamite, but faulty wiring caused a shattering explosion that tore the roof off the building, killed two of the gang, and drove the hostages and the four surviving terrorists into the street and the arms of the police.

Other gang exploits included a joint attack with Arab terrorists upon a Jewish old-people's home in Munich, which left seven dead. In 1977 the gang kidnapped, then murdered, the industrialist Hanns-Martin Schleyer. For a few years Baader-Meinhof faded from view. Then early in the 1980s the terrorists leaped into the headlines

Dringend gesuchte Terroristen

Im Zusammenhang mit dem

- dreifachen Mord an Generalbundesanwalt Buback und zwei seiner Begleiter am 7. 4. 1977 in Karlsruhe

- Mord an Jürgen Ponto am 30. 7. 1977 in Oberursel

- vierfachen Mord und der Entführung von Hanns-Martin Schleyer am 5. 9. 1977 in Köln

werden gesucht:

A West German police poster distributed worldwide in seven languages, with photos of terrorists wanted for the murder of the industrialist Hanns-Martin Schleyer in 1977.

again. In 1981 they used car bombs in several attacks upon U.S. Air Force personnel in Germany. One such explosion injured twenty people. In Heidelberg they ambushed the car of General Frederick J. Kroesen, the U.S. Army's European commander. They wounded him and his wife by firing an antitank grenade from wooded hills at his car. In June 1982 the terrorists exploded bombs at four U.S. military bases, damaging the buildings.

Some of the German terrorists experienced a change of heart and mind. Hans-Joachim Klein was wounded while helping to kidnap OPEC ministers in Vienna in 1975. Later he gave up terrorism because "the demented actions of international terrorists" were "enough to make me puke—above all, it made me think. . . . I have changed back to a person with sensible political thinking and behavior. . . . I had to pay a hell of a price." Asked if he felt guilty, he answered, "Guilty is not a strong enough word. I feel that I shall be covered in shit for the rest of my days. It is my own shit because I believed blindly in what I was doing." How did it happen? "You begin by giving up your humanity," he said, "and end by renouncing your political ideals. The relation between your objective and the means used to reach it becomes insane."

One of the Baader-Meinhof gang's founders and leaders, Horst Mahler, came to a like conclusion. From prison, where he was serving a long sentence for robbing banks to finance terrorist operations, he wrote: "We refuse to justify the murder of unarmed civilians, massacres, kidnappings, as a form of anti-imperialist struggle. Acts like these are crimes against the revolution."

By the end of 1982 some forty terrorists and their supporters had been brought to trial in West Germany. Eleven of them are serving life sentences. Another twenty were still believed to be at large.

Chapter 12

The Millionaire Revolutionary

It's hard to take a millionaire revolutionary seriously.

Yet that's what one of Italy's leading terrorists was.

He was born in 1926 to one of Europe's wealthiest families. He ended his life one night in 1972, burned and mutilated when the dynamite sticks he was taping to a high-tension tower outside Milan exploded in his inexpert hands.

Twenty-four hours later the police discovered that the dead man was Giangiacomo Feltrinelli, heir to an immense Milanese fortune and head of one of Europe's most distinguished publishing houses. In the Volkswagen Feltrinelli had parked near the tower, the police found maps marked with the sites of other power pylons, bridges, airports, military barracks. Raids on his hideouts uncovered arsenals of weapons and ammunition, dynamite, forged passports, stolen identity cards, coded letters, radio receivers tuned to police frequen-

The body of Giangiacomo Feltrinelli, millionaire Italian publisher, found burned and mutilated on the ground near a high tension tower outside Milan. He was killed when the dynamite he was taping to the tower blew up in his hands.

cies, lists of people in political, financial, and industrial circles tagged for possible kidnapping.

It was years before all the facts about Feltrinelli's role in international terrorist operations came to light. His family owned huge timber tracts, cattle ranches, banks, real estate, industry. The boy was raised like a prince, kept from others of his age, isolated in a grand house full of servants. His stepfather, the writer Luigi Barzini, wrote of him:

> From his lonely and harshly disciplined childhood, he inherited a curious incapacity to tolerate any form of control, to distinguish between people or behave as if others were his equals. He could be deferential with superiors and arrogant with inferiors, was seldom courteous and matter-of-fact with his peers. He ended by preferring always the company of the illiterate, the fanatic, and those who were in some way dependent upon him.

As a teenager, said Barzini, Feltrinelli became an ardent admirer of Mussolini, parading the house in a fascist uniform. Then a gardener converted him to the revolution, and he joined the Communist underground in 1942. When the Allied armies invaded Italy in 1944, Feltrinelli fought with the liberation forces.

After the war Feltrinelli created a foundation bearing his name that documented European working-class movements. He started a publishing house to encourage new writers on the left, and published illustrious novels such as Boris Pasternak's *Dr. Zhivago* and Giuseppe di Lampedusa's *The Leopard*. He was also the first to print an Italian edition of Marighella's *Mini-Manual* as well as other radical literature. When the Russians objected to his issuing the banned work of Pasternak, Feltrinelli resigned from the Italian Communist party. It "has disappointed me," he said.

Now he joined a secret band of former partisans, the Flying Red Squad. They refused to go along with the Communists' readiness to work with nonrevolutionary parties in the capitalist state. They used violence against fascists and communists alike, robbing banks to fund their operations.

After Castro's victory in Cuba Feltrinelli paid many visits to see how the new communist society was working. He took part there in the Tricontinental Conference of 1966, at which Third World groups called for a "global revolutionary strategy to counter the global strategy of American imperialism." Soon afterward Cuba opened a chain of training camps for guerrilla fighters. Palestinians flew in to learn lessons they taught in turn in their own Middle Eastern training centers. By the 1970s such camps were located in Soviet Russia and its satellites as well as in the newly liberated African nations of Angola, Mozambique, Algeria, and Libya. Through these camps passed an incredible variety of fighters for utopian societies they never clearly defined.

In several of Italy's largest cities Feltrinelli opened a chain of bookstores offering everything from quality literature to the *Mini-Manual* of terrorism and Feltrinelli's own newspaper, *The Left*. While he could make stump speeches during a May 1968 upheaval in the Italian universities, he could also appear in *Vogue* magazine to model the latest fashion in men's furs. He continued to enjoy the millionaire's life—two yachts, custom-built cars, a villa on Lake Garda, a mansion in the mountains, a hunting lodge in the Austrian forest. All that while writing and publishing a document called *Italy 1968: Political Guerrilla Warfare*. In it he said that what Italy badly needed was to provoke the state into revealing its "reactionary essence." The job of the revolutionary was to "violate the law openly . . . challenging and outraging institutions and public order in every way. Then, when the state intervenes as a result, with police and the courts, it will be easy to denounce its harshness and repressive dictatorial tendencies." He urged militants to work with anybody to throw the government off-balance—with ethnic and regional minorities and even right-wing terrorists. And whatever their methods—even to killing innocent victims indiscriminately.

As though they had eavesdropped on Feltrinelli, right-wing terrorists began to act in just that way. They bombed crowded banks, outdoor rallies, and Italy's express trains. Such unselective violence, Feltrinelli now wrote, would help force "an authoritarian turn to the right, opening a more advanced phase of struggle." As the government cracked down on terrorism, he added, the people would come to see that no "socialist revolution is possible without resorting to arms."

The judge assigned to investigate Feltrinelli's death, Guido Viola, concluded that he was possessed of the idea of bringing on a right-wing coup in Italy. "He awaited it, desired it, almost invoked it, so as to lead the guerrilla resistance" he hoped would follow it.

After the Havana conference, Feltrinelli went to Beirut and offered the PFLP leader, George Habash, the funds to carry his terrorism into Europe. He also met with Horst Mahler and Ulrike Meinhof to discuss revolutionary strategy. In Berlin on May Day 1968, standing beside Mahler and Meinhof, he made a speech calling for armed violence. In France and Italy he recruited young people for training in Habash's Middle East camps. He opened a secret account in a Swiss bank to fund a central organization in Zurich that would channel cash, weapons, and services to international terrorist groups.

Then late in 1969 Feltrinelli vanished underground, living under false names for the last two years of his life. He founded the Proletarian Action Group (GAP) to prepare for "armed struggles against the bosses and fascist pigs." One of Italy's first left-wing terrorist bands, its recruits were trained in mountain camps, given weapons and lessons in bombing, arson, robbery, kidnapping, and killing. In those final years Feltrinelli adopted the style of the Tupamaros, growing a bushy mustache and wearing their military uniform. For GAP he set up many safehouses and gathered great stocks of weapons. His group claimed credit for dozens of bombings and arson attacks upon factories and army barracks as well as Italy's first terrorist kidnapping for money. Feltrinelli's targets were diverse and widespread—the Israeli port of Haifa, the U.S. embassy in Athens, banks in Milan and Genoa. In 1971 he went to Uruguay to watch the Tupamaros at work. That same year he organized an international conference in a Jesuit college in Florence, attended by terrorist groups from Italy, Germany, Ireland, Argentina, Turkey, Palestine, and eight other countries. Their aim was to coordinate plans for international terrorist action.

Later that year he proposed to other revolutionary groups that a joint high command be set up for an underground Army of National Liberation. When street riots broke out in Milan a few months later, he was with the mob hurling stones at the windows of an establishment newspaper.

It was GAP that gave its first supply of dynamite to the Red Brigades, which would soon become known as one of Italy's sensational terrorist groups. The years after Feltrinelli's death saw a fantastic rise in terrorism. In 1979 alone 2,750 terrorist assaults were recorded in Italy, claimed by 215 left-wing groups.

But the terrorism was by no means the work solely of leftists. Fascist groups used violence with the same objectives. They hoped to create panic and chaos so that their people could seize power through a coup. The very first large-scale terrorist attack in Italy came in 1969, when right-wing militants exploded a bomb in a public square in Milan that killed fourteen and injured eighty. It was to combat the fascists that left-wing groups such as the Red Brigades took to the streets. They believed that the right's terrorism was being used by the security forces to discredit the left. Revelations by the courts and the press pointed to close connections between the police and the fascists.

No wonder cynicism soured Italian life. Ever since the war Italy's government had been an ever-changing chaos of bureaucracy and inefficiency. Italians suspected everyone of corruption. The young, still hopeful of a better Italy, looked to the left for leadership. Italy's Communist party was large and powerful in the trade unions. But the young militants saw the party as too accommodating, too passive, too willing to compromise with the government in power, too indifferent to revolutionary change. They denounced party leaders for selling out the workers in exchange for cabinet posts. The Communist party became furiously hostile to such destructive groups as the Red Brigades. It feared they would cripple negotiations it was conducting to break its isolation from mainstream politics.

It was at this point that the Red Brigades chose to kidnap Aldo Moro, the man most responsible for negotiating an alliance between the Communists and the Catholics, another great political power of Italy. Moro was a Christian Democrat who had been Prime Minister and was slated to be Italy's next president. One March morning in 1978 a Brigade squad ambushed Moro's car, killed his five bodyguards, and abducted Moro. They held him prisoner for 54 days, conducting a mock trial through the press while they demanded the release of Red Brigade prisoners in an exchange for Moro. When the government refused to make a deal, they murdered Moro and dumped his bullet-riddled body in the trunk of a car, which they left on a street in Rome midway between the headquarters of the Communists and the Christian Democrats.

By now the Red Brigades had several hundred men and women operating in secret units in Rome, Venice, Milan, Turin, Genoa, and Naples. They could count on sympathizers for shelter and assistance, and bank robberies for funds. Rival groups—new splinters from the old left—appeared to challenge their supremacy in terrorism. A fresh wave of attacks began in 1980. Terrorists raided a business school in Turin, picked out five teachers and five students, and shot them in the legs as a warning not to become "servants" of the multinational corporations. Factory workers were murdered, police officers shot dead in the streets. In August came the most atrocious terrorist assault in postwar Europe. A time bomb exploded in the railway station at Bologna. It killed 84 people and wounded 200 more. It was the job of a right-wing group.

The security forces, reorganized and strengthened after the murder of Moro, rounded up 240 left-wing and ninety right-wing terrorists during 1980 and sent them to prison. In their raids on hideouts the police seized 6,000 weapons and 350,000 rounds of ammunition, together with explosives, mortars, and grenade throwers. That year 1,264 terrorist attacks were reported, a significant drop from the record 2,395 of 1978.

The next year the Red Brigades kidnapped U.S. Brigadier General James Dozier from his Verona apartment. The police found him in Padua 42 days later. They freed him unharmed and captured five armed terrorists. The rescue gave signs of a weakening of terrorist morale, for the police were led to Dozier by tips from captured or defecting members of the group. During the police hunt for Dozier nearly 400 Red Brigade suspects were seized throughout Italy, and seventeen of them were charged in the kidnapping. One of them was 27-year-old Antonio Savasta, son of a Rome policeman, who had organized the kidnapping. He was charged with a direct or indirect role in a total of seventeen murders by the Red Brigades, including Moro's killing. He said in a court deposition that his group had made contact with the PLO right after the murder of Moro. Another captured Brigades member, Patrizio Peci, said the PLO had supplied his group with arms.

At the Dozier trial Savasta recanted his years in the armed underground and urged those in hiding to surrender. Explaining why he was informing on his terrorist comrades, he told the court: "The armed struggle is in a crisis. We took up arms to resolve the problems of the crisis, of unemployment, of tendency toward war." At the trial's end, the court sentenced the terrorists to prison terms ranging from 26 months to 27 years. After his confession, which implicated all the other gang members, Savasta circulated a handwritten statement: "Today," it said, "and this is part of the self-criticism, we realized that we set in motion a machine, and just like pure adventurists, representatives of the most infantile extremism. If we do not stop it now, it will crush everything."

Earlier, another Red Brigades prisoner, Enrico Fenzi,

To prevent attempts at rescue, members of the Red Brigades, the Italian terrorist group, are held in steel cages in the courtroom during their trial on charges of kidnappings and murders.

wrote from his prison cell: "The armed struggle failed in all the political and social goals that it set for itself for ten years. One must have the courage to refuse it totally; if not, one condemns oneself to madness."

Does the outcome of the Moro and Dozier trials mean that terror in Italy is ended? Such optimism is not warranted, writes Henry Kamm, *The New York Times* correspondent who covered the Dozier case:

> Terrorist groups on both the right and left have often succeeded in returning defiantly to action, even after important cells of activists have been captured or turned themselves in. Moreover, the mood that produced many of these groups—drift, cynical bravado and disillusionment with the Establishment—remains prevalent among Italian youth. . . .
>
> Concern remains that the frustration of life in what leftists like to describe as a "blocked society" remains compelling among many well-educated young people. Such sentiments, stimulated by the example of the brigades' glory days, could give rise to new waves of terrorism, under the Red Brigades' flag or another name.

A few months after he wrote that, the Brigades claimed credit for shooting two policemen in Rome. The officers apparently were lured from their patrol car into a dark alley, disarmed, made to kneel down, and shot in the head. A message sent by the Brigades to the press said: "We caught and annihilated the police patrol. With the Moro trial the state is trying to destroy ten years of proletarian struggles."

Chapter 13

Up Against the Wall

It happened late one March morning in 1970, on a quiet row of handsome town houses in New York's Greenwich Village.

Five young people were in the house at 18 West Eleventh Street when a tremendous roar that could be heard for blocks shattered the noon stillness. Much of the house collapsed instantly, smoke, dust, and debris filling the air. Two more blasts followed as the gas mains burst into flames. People came running and screaming out of the buildings nearby. Inside the exploded house Theodore Gold, 23, Diane Oughton, 28, and Terry Robins, 21, died at once. Ted's body was found late that night, crushed and mangled under heavy beams. Fragments of Diana's body were gathered together and identified four days later. There was no part of Terry left big enough to be identified. His death in the blast was

A poster carried in a political demonstration refers to Oughton, Gold, and Robins of the Weather Underground, killed in New York in 1970 when their bomb factory blew up.

determined only by a message from the underground.

The two others, Cathlyn Wilkerson, 25, and Kathy Boudin, 26, were probably in the front of the house asleep when the blast went off. Both survived the explosion and were seen running away. They disappeared.

What had happened in that house?

The five were members of a small terrorist group known as the Weather Underground. They were staying in the home of James P. Wilkerson, a wealthy owner of radio stations, while he was away on a Caribbean vacation. In his absence his daughter Cathlyn had allowed her fellow terrorists to use the basement of the house as a bomb factory. On the shelves and floor of the makeshift workshop were piles of explosives, at least 100 sticks of dynamite, some packed into twelve-inch lead-pipe bombs and others into tape-wrapped packages. All around were detonating caps, batteries, wires, alarm clocks to be used as timing devices. A few minutes before noon Terry and Diana must have connected a wrong wire to the one more bomb they were making. . . .

The two survivors of that tragic explosion disappeared underground. In 1980 Cathlyn gave herself up and began serving time on a charge connected with the explosion of her father's townhouse.

Kathy Boudin stayed underground. Eleven years after the Eleventh Street bombing she was captured, along with several others, as she fled from the robbery of the Brink's armored car in Nyack, New York, in which a Brink's guard and two policemen were shot to death.

A bitter-end holdout, she was still living in her own political nightmare.

The Weather Underground came out of the radicalism of the 1960s. The action began in the South when Blacks took up the struggle to end segregation and discrimination. Those protests soon spread to Northern cities as whites joined with Blacks in demonstrations against discrimination in jobs, housing, education, social services. It moved to the schools and colleges, which became the focus of bitter confrontations and rising radical demands.

Many of the young radicals were the children of parents who had experienced the trials of the Great Depression and World War II, and who were now enjoying economic security and material comfort, often for the first time. These middle-class children chafed at suburban dullness and smugness. Learning about poverty and racism in the ghettoes of the North as well as the South, they hoped that the Kennedy administration of the early 1960s would move toward a society of greater freedom and equality and find a way to live in peace with the other great power, Soviet Russia.

But Kennedy's support of covert attempts to abort rebellions in the underdeveloped nations, and his increasing involvement in the Vietnam War, deepened a growing mood of frustration and powerlessness. The rock and folk music of the time began to reflect that feeling. The young radicals rejected getting and spending as a way of life. They wanted to restore warmth and simplicity to human relationships. Many turned to a communal mode of living, ready to share all their possessions. The ideal was a life of peace and love. But feeling good, with or without chemical assistance, was not enough, said the radical activists. The poor and oppressed were still poor and oppressed. You must act— not just talk or dream—to change the world.

And many of the New Left did. Hundreds of young people journeyed South in the summer of 1963 to help Blacks struggle for their rights as citizens and their dignity as human beings. They responded to the appeal of the Reverend Martin Luther King, Jr., for nonviolent action to achieve integration. And through the Student Nonviolent Coordinating Committee they shared a fraternity of black and white that would last all too briefly.

The Northern movement for civil rights centered at first around the Students for a Democratic Society (SDS). It grew from a few dozen activists in 1962 to a peak of about 8,000 core members in 1968, with another 75,000 students loosely connected to hundreds of campus chapters. It was SDS that set the tone of the early New Left. Its program pledged SDS to the creation of a New Left around ethical values like fraternity, honesty, and love. It attacked reliance on threats of war as the heart of foreign policy, and promised to crack through public indifference to the dangerous course of the "military-industrial complex" President Eisenhower had warned against. The SDS had no faith in the Marxist axiom that the working class would transform capitalism into socialism. Instead of a workers' revolt, the SDS called for a "democracy of individual participation." By that it meant a way of living in which all people would share in making the important decisions that shape their lives. SDS took the first practical steps toward that end by trying to promote self-organization of the people in the ghettoes.

SDS had no trouble spotting social problems, but solving them proved to be far harder. Despite some successes the ghetto organizing soon fell apart. Calls for radical action left most of the country cold. For there was no left movement of any substance in the U.S., as there was in Europe. The labor movement was declining in strength. Its members fought for more money in the pay envelope, not to overthrow the government. They were not class conscious; their goal was to rise into the middle class and enjoy all its material benefits. The political parties of the old left—the Socialists, the Communists, and their many splinter sects—had failed to take hold in America. Who even remembered what they had stood for? And the New Left had no interest in learning from the mistakes of the old. As for the Blacks— the major victims of oppression—they soon showed they wanted to go it alone, without the aid of white radicals.

So the SDS turned for support to the young—and students especially. The leaders theorized that the university was the real basis and agency for a movement of radical change. And at first the militancy that flared on the campus gave them the illusion they were right. The first student uprising broke out at the University of California in Berkeley in 1964. And soon campus confrontations with authority became commonplace, with the SDS the prime mover. At Berkeley it was a free speech issue that galvanized the students. There were demonstrations, tangles with police, bangs and bruises, arrests, a no-going-to-class strike, and finally the lifting of free speech restrictions. Although a new and more responsive university administration took over, the student militants were still defiant. Once the free speech issue was resolved at Berkeley, however, student support for radical action began to fade.

But not for long. America became entangled in the war in Vietnam, and the tide of militancy rose on campuses throughout the country. It was pushed even higher by the SDS campaign against the draft and American involvement in the war. Marches and rallies at first, then sit-ins, draft card burnings, and other forms of protest. As the sixties wore on, some SDSers looked to the urban guerrillas abroad for a new pattern of resistance. They too would launch a struggle to liberate America, and take to the streets to fight it out. The painfully slow and difficult—if not impossible—goal of participatory democracy failed as a guiding ethic. Fidel Castro, Ché Guevara—Third World liberation heroes—became the models for the most militant of the young.

Thousands of protesters besieged the centers where young draftees were inducted into the Army. It took riot police to break up a sit-in at Dow, makers of napalm, a chemical component of bombs being used in

Vietnam. At the Democratic National Convention in 1968 Chicago's frenzied police force assaulted antiwar demonstrators and bystanders alike with clubs, tear gas and Mace. Hundreds were arrested and hundreds more injured badly.

In the first half of 1968 there were over 200 major demonstrations involving over 40,000 students on 100 campuses. That spring Columbia University enjoyed, or suffered, the most spectacular of them all. The SDS demanded that the university divorce itself from a campus institute doing military research, while black students protested Columbia's real estate operations in the surrounding ghetto. The two groups invaded and occupied campus buildings until the police took them back by storm. About 700 students were arrested and 150 injured. When the other students struck in sympathy, the university closed down for the remainder of the spring semester.

The battle made heroes of SDS leaders like Mark Rudd, but the membership shrank as he and 72 other students were suspended. Headline happy from the international attention the uprising won, and dizzy with visions of themselves as young Lenins, the SDS leaders expected to meet the revolution around the corner. Instead, the organization began to fall apart. Anarchists, Maoists, Stalinists, Trotskyites, all tried to force SDS into their own mold. The movement was torn by factional quarrels and doctrinal disputes. It became smaller and smaller as it failed to find new followers. It was still, in the late sixties—much as student movements were in Europe and Latin America—made up largely of white middle-class students. And they had no connection with the mass of Americans. Julius Lester, a black activist, pointed out their basic weakness:

> The student radical is never heard talking about a rise in the price of milk, new taxes, real wages, or doctor bills. The student radical creates his own society in which money is not an overriding problem, and because it isn't, the student radical thinks that revolution is all about love, because he has time to think about love. Everybody else is thinking about survival.

But weak as SDS really was, the attention the widespread student disturbances got in the media made many people fear a Red flag would soon wave over the White House. Richard Nixon won office that fall on a pledge to restore "law and order," and once in power began to violate the Constitution himself to crack down on dissidents. SDS became the main target of attack and was banned on many campuses.

In this tense atmosphere the SDS met in Chicago in June 1969 for its ninth (and last) annual convention. A statement distributed by a handful of the most militant called for immediate revolutionary action. This group became known as the Weathermen, a term taken from a song by Bob Dylan. The Weathermenbelieved they could build an army of guerrilla fighters by the symbolic power of violence on the streets of America. The only way to change the country was through violent confrontation. Put people up against the wall, they said, force them to choose, and they'll have to be either for the revolution or for the system.

That marked the decisive break in SDS. The Weathermen pulled out, effectively putting an end to SDS. The Weathermen had already dismissed working-class whites and the middle class as bought off or brainwashed. To whom could they turn for guerrilla fighters? To the alienated young, they decided. Motorcycle gangs, high school dropouts, rock freaks, street kids—these would be their Red Army. And the way to show them that university radicals were not softies was to pick fights with teenage gangs, on the streets or in the schools. They tried it in Detroit on a beach and were badly beaten up. In Pittsburgh they roared through a high school's corridors yelling "Jailbreak!" It didn't revolutionize anyone, but got 26 Weatherwomen arrested. They raided a building at Harvard, beating up an instructor and a librarian, to prove how tough they were. They summoned thousands to a national action in Chicago they called "Days of Rage," but scarcely 200 showed. They rampaged through the streets, smashing windows in stores, cars, banks, apartment houses until the police broke up the riot and arrested many of them.

The results? Only popular disgust. "We have to get into armed struggle," said one of their leaders, Bernadine Dohrn. She announced that the Weathermen were adapting "the Tupamaros classic guerrilla strategy." The group called a meeting in Michigan, to which they invited potential recruits, including a number between the ages of thirteen and sixteen. There Dohrn talked to them about the recent mass murder in California committed by Charles Manson and his gang. Praising the gang's "revolutionary" sadism, she said, "Dig it, first they killed those pigs, then they ate dinner in the same room with them, then they even shoved a fork into a victim's stomach! Wild!"

Mark Rudd, media star of the Columbia uprising, told the recruits, "It's a wonderful feeling to hit a pig [cop]. It must be a really wonderful feeling to kill a pig or blow up a building." Another Weatherman added, "We're against anything that's 'good and decent' in honky America. We will burn and loot and destroy."

Something had gone terribly wrong. Many of the Weathermen had once been compassionate young people, eager to end racism and poverty and injustice, hoping to make a society dedicated to love and dignity, not power and profit. How did someone committed to human liberation through peaceful means turn into a fanatical advocate of terrorism?

Just before the Weathermen went completely underground, they issued a public statement:

> The notion of public violence is increasingly key. . . . We have to answer all the pig sounds about sabotage being terrible, suicidal and adventurous with what we have learned from the Vietnamese and from black revolutionaries. . . . Armed struggle starts when someone starts it. . . . To debate about the "correct time and conditions" to begin the fight, or about a phase of work necessary to prepare the people for the revolution is reactionary. MAKING WAR on the state creates both

the consciousness and conditions for the expansion of the struggle.

Then, in another message after disappearing underground:

> Our job is to lead white kids to armed revolution. . . . Tens of thousands have learned that protest and marches won't do it. Revolutionary violence is the only way.

In March 1970 came the town house explosion on Eleventh Street in New York. Three of the Weather Underground were blown up while making bombs designed to be used against people, not buildings. Two days before the blast, Kathy Boudin, who escaped and disappeared underground, had told David Dellinger, a movement friend, of her fears that the Weatherpeople were losing touch with "the revolutionary love" that had motivated them to embark on their new course of terrorism.

The town house disaster didn't stop the bombings. In New York the terrorists planted bombs in banks, office buildings, piers. In Wisconsin they raided and vandalized draft board offices, Army Reserve headquarters, and ROTC installations. They bombed the home of a judge presiding over a Black Panther trial. After inmates at Attica penitentiary in New York state were massacred in a prison uprising, they bombed the Department of Corrections office in Albany. They bombed the central headquarters of the New York City Police Department, two buildings of the California prison authority, the computer room in the Pentagon, the Capitol Building in Washington. They chose their targets as symbols of power and to demonstrate the government's vulnerability to attack. And they often gave advance warning to avoid human injury.

But they failed to weaken the government or rouse the people to revolutionary action. All they succeeded in doing was getting most Americans to detest them, even many who were once their friends and allies.

The road to terrorism has been taken by other groups in the United States, and for quite different causes. In the spring of 1982 bomb blasts hit Wall Street, damaging several large buildings that house stock exchanges and banks. The explosions marked the resurgence of the FALN, a Puerto Rican terrorist group. They acted in the name of revolutionary independence for Puerto Rico. Back in 1950 Puerto Rican terrorists had tried but failed to murder President Harry Truman. In 1954 they entered the Capitol and shot and wounded five congressmen. Little was heard of them again until, in 1973, they placed incendiary devices in New York department stores, and the next year exploded powerful bombs at several business sites in the city. Early in 1975 they bombed a luncheon club in the Fraunces Tavern of New York (where General George Washington had bid farewell to his Revolutionary War officers), killing three people and injuring forty. In the next months their explosives shook banks, an insurance company, restaurants, office buildings, and corporate headquarters in New York, Chicago, and Washington.

Yet no mass support among Puerto Ricans was evidenced for any of the violence. A minority of Puerto Ricans supported independence, but neither those on the island nor those on the mainland showed enthusiasm for terrorist attempts to force it.

Nothing gained as much publicity for terrorism as the kidnapping of Patricia (Patty) Hearst in 1974. The nineteen-year-old Berkeley student was the granddaughter of the late William Randolph Hearst, builder of a huge publishing empire. She was abducted from her apartment at gunpoint by three men and five women who called themselves the Symbionese Liberation Army. Little had been heard of the SLA until the Hearst kidnapping. The SLA members were, all but one, children of white middle-class families, and college educated. Searching for means to bring about revolutionary change, they met through a common interest in penal reform. Blacks made up a majority of the prisoners in California, and they felt a need to do something to atone for white society's racism. When Donald DeFreeze, one of the black prisoners they visited, escaped, they hid him from the police. He became their leader. Soon after, some of the group murdered Marcus Foster, a black superintendent of schools in Oakland. Foster, they said, had let the police patrol the schools to guard against violence.

A few months later the SLA kidnapped Patty Hearst because her family was the symbol of hated Big Business. At first she was assaulted and abused, but then she joined her captors and shared their outlaw life. She took part in two bank robberies, other thefts, and sev-

Patty Hearst, granddaughter of the founder of the Hearst publishing empire, was kidnapped by a terrorist group in 1974. She joined them in bank robberies and bombings and was sent to prison.

eral bombings. She stayed underground after DeFreeze and five others of the gang were killed in a shoot-out with the police. Arrested by the FBI sixteen months later, Hearst was found guilty of armed bank robbery and sent to prison. It was a rapid end to a pathetic conspiracy.

Terrorism by organized hate groups rarely gained the headlines of a Patty Hearst. Nevertheless, the painful record of bigots using violence began to swell in the late 1970s and has continued into the 1980s. Racist and anti-Semitic groups committed outrages in communities all across the nation. The upsurge in terrorism on the right was linked in part to the revival of the Ku Klux Klan and several neo-Nazi groups. Although total Klan membership in the U.S., was estimated at 10,000 in 1982, perhaps another 100,000 could be considered active sympathizers, judging by attendance at Klan rallies, subscribers to Klan literature, and Gallup polls.

The organized bigots are responsible for assaults and conspiracies against Blacks, Jews, Hispanics, Asians, and other minorities, using clubs, guns, and bombs. They have established paramilitary camps for children in several places to train followers in the use of weapons, demolitions, and guerrilla tactics.

Besides the Klan, other active hate groups include splintered neo-Nazi organizations: the National Socialist White People's Party, the National Socialist Party of America, and the National Socialist White Worker's Party. Another group, the National States Rights Party, is a hybrid of neo-Nazi and Klan elements. There is also a Christian Patriots Defense League, which limits itself to "White Christian Americans" and calls for race wars.

Like Marighella's *Mini-Manual* for terrorists of the left is *The Turner Diaries*, a blueprint for revolution by the American right. It provides details on explosives, military tactics, supplies, logistics, and potential targets for terrorism. Anyone who opposes racism, it concludes, must be hanged.

Chapter 14

The Terrorist State

However chilling the atrocities of terrorist groups, they pale beside the systematic terrorism inflicted by governments on their own people.

Evil is evil. You can't measure it in pounds or inches. Whether evil is done to one human being or to a million, it is still evil. But a government has enormously greater power to do violence to its citizens than a small band of terrorists.

In the years 1968–78, terrorist groups worldwide killed about 10,000 people. In its first year in power in Argentina (1976–77) the military dictatorship almost equaled that number. Such gradations of terrorism are worth attention.

States throughout history have used terroristic acts of violence to systematically put down groups or individuals, or to frighten their whole people into doing whatever the government wants. Back in the time of the Caesars, Nero was but one of the Roman emperors who ruled by terrorism. He killed members of his own family and the families of anyone else who displeased him. He slaughtered the nobility and set fire to Rome. Everyone was an enemy to him. And in his power and madness he made them all victims of his terrorism.

We saw earlier how mass terror was used during the French Revolution as the weapon of factions against one another and ultimately against all the French. Violent repression, then as now, was arbitrary, unpredictable, and indiscriminate. Under modern authoritarian or totalitarian regimes it becomes the job of specialized agencies of the state. Every one of them—whether Hitler's Germany, Stalin's Russia, or Mao's China—seems unable to do without a secret police force it trains in the methods of murder, torture, forced confessions, denunciation. Their job is to hunt down dissenters, political or cultural. To imprison or kill those labeled enemies of the state or the revolution. To spin a web of informers in every corner of the land. To censor thought, to force conformity.

In such regimes terrorism is usually employed first against the people or classes formerly in power. Then it may be directed against members of the party now in power who no longer agree with policy—the "opposition," quickly tagged "traitors" or "counterrevolutionaries." Later, ethnic groups or religious minorities may become the victims of terror.

When Hitler took office in Germany early in 1933,

his first move was to consolidate his power. He banned demonstrations, suspended all civil rights, wiped out the non-Nazi press. His Secret State Police, the Gestapo, was authorized to arrest and even execute any suspicious person. Thousands were jailed, beaten, tortured to death. Quickly he succeeded in suppressing all expression of independent thought and eliminating all opposition. He borrowed the idea of concentration camps from the Russians and ordered the Gestapo to confine in them anyone it pleased, without trial or conviction. It was mass control by terror. The Jews became a special target of that terrorism.

Historians of Hitler's twelve-year rule of terror estimate that the victims of his gassing, gallows, firing squads, and other means of murder totalled between 10 and 12 million. (Six million of these were Jews. The rest were other minorities: ethnic, such as Gypsies; political, such as Communists; and other "misfits," such as homosexuals.) This estimate does not count those lost in battle or bombings.

To calculate the number in Soviet Russia who fell victim to the terrorism of that totalitarian society is difficult. Beginning with Lenin's seizure of power in 1917, and going to Stalin's death in 1953, scholars estimate that from 40 to 50 million people passed through Soviet jails or slave labor camps. Those who died there—by execution, hunger, or disease—totaled 15 to 25 million. At any one time in Stalin's regime, as many as 6 million political prisoners were held in Soviet jails or concentration camps. In *The Gulag Archipelago* Alexander Solzhenitsyn provides evidence that during 1937–38—the height of Stalin's terror—half a million political prisoners were shot throughout the country.

Within a year of Stalin's death a relaxation of the policy of mass terror was observed. Many political prisoners were released from the labor camps and prisons. But in the years that followed, the Soviet government crushed movements for more open socialist societies among its satellites—East Germany, Czechoslovakia, Hungary, Poland—and it became clear the monolithic system left no room for human freedom. Though mass repressions are avoided today, labor camps still exist. The threat of terror hangs over the Soviet people, making fear the right arm of the rulers.

Communist China too, after thirty years in power, admitted its use of terrorism against its own citizens. Soon after the death of Mao, the Communist leadership exposed the existence of political persecution of innocent people. The Chinese press carried accounts of widespread arbitrary detention. Brutal interrogation methods were used, including mental and physical torture.

Another Communist regime, Cambodia, was ruled by the Khmer Rouge for nearly four years (until the Vietnamese army overthrew it in 1979). The Khmer Rouge imposed a system of nationwide forced labor. Murder and the threat of murder were the means of control. In a land of 7 million people it was estimated that over 1 million died as a result of terrorism. It was a case of genocide by the regime against its own people.

Before African liberation, the European colonial powers exploiting that continent relied on terrorism to keep down national movements. But since liberation many of the new African states, according to Amnesty International, have themselves used terrorism against internal political dissidents or to suppress religious or racial groups. Uganda under the dictator Idi Amin was perhaps the worst example. During his period in power (1971–79) his wildly unpredictable, random methods of killing cost the lives of over 100,000 Ugandans.

Terrorism dominates the lives of many millions of Latin Americans. Five countries—Argentina, Bolivia, Chile, Paraguay, and Uruguay—make up a solid block of cruelly repressive power. Violation of human rights in all of them is appallingly commonplace. Let's take Argentina as but one example of the use of terrorism by the military dictatorships on the southern cone of the continent. Robert Cox, who for years edited a newspaper in Buenos Aires, said of Argentina:

> In the 1970s, Argentina became a laboratory of terror. The country was subjected to the most extreme onslaught of terrorism ever unleashed upon any developed nation—first from the left and then from the right. And finally, Argentina became what can only be called a terrorist state. This total terrorism has had a devastating effect upon society, poisoning everything.

In 1976 the military seized power in Argentina. It disbanded Congress and suspended all political activity, placing the country's 26 million citizens under martial law. The coup was no surprise. For twenty years Argentina had been the scene of a continuous struggle between weak civilian governments and a powerful military. There were constant outbreaks of violence by fifty different bands of terrorists, viewed by some at first as romantic guerrillas. They carried out bombings, assassinations, kidnappings, and even full-scale battles.

After the coup the terror continued, only now through armed violence by the right, with the silent consent or cooperation of the junta. Bloody episodes that the press had reported before the coup could no longer be presented to the public eye: the appearance of bodies in ditches and rivers; mutilated corpses on garbage heaps and in burned-out cars; the "disappearances" of scores, then hundreds, and finally thousands of people after they had been abducted by armed men who presented themselves as members of the security forces.

The military government had taken over the reins of power with the promise to restore law and order. But these "disappearances" continued from 1976 through 1981. The number then began to lessen considerably, partly because of pressure from human rights groups in Argentina and abroad.

The Argentine tragedy, says Cox, "stems largely from the failure of ordinary people to respond with revulsion when confronted with inhumanity." From the very beginning of the violence, he points out, before the military took power, decent people rationalized or justified much that should be unacceptable by all civilized standards:

> Perfectly reasonable people saw reasonability in the actions of the terrorists. It was only to be expected, they argued, that foreign businessmen should be kidnapped for ransom. It was the only way their multinational companies could be made to pay the taxes they could avoid under the legal system. When Argentine businessmen became the terrorists' targets, people reasoned that the victims were all special cases, guilty of exploiting their workers, perhaps, or of profiteering. When the terrorists began picking off policemen and military officers . . . the victims were again dehumanized by the speculation that they must have been torturers or have been involved in some kind of dirty work.

Cox does not find it at all surprising, therefore, that:

> Today many of the same people justify the state's terrorist methods on much the same grounds. Anyone who "disappears" must be a subversive, they say. The apathy of public opinion in Argentina, allied with a pernicious facility for rationalizing criminal behavior on the part of the country's intellectuals, created a situation in which terrorists—first from the left and then from the right (and undoubtedly, forming part of the apparatus of the security forces)—have been able to operate, at various times, with immunity and impunity.
>
> Today the conservative conscience is as complacent about the enormous human suffering in Argentina as the

revolutionary left was unconcerned about the misery it was causing at the height of the terrorist onslaught.

What he learned from his experience in Argentina, says Cox, is that terrorism can get so powerful a grip on a society that the police and armed forces "are driven mad by the ferocity of the enemy." They fail to resist the temptation to retaliate in the same brutal way, which makes all humankind the loser.

Even when the terrorists are defeated, they win in the sense that they have made democracy and decency the loser. What happened in Argentina is being repeated in other countries of the continent, Central America especially. In Nicaragua, El Salvador, Guatemala, terrorists of the right and of the left use murder almost as an end in itself.

Studying El Salvador, the Mexican social critic Gabriel Zaid concludes it is another of those bloody and ruthless struggles between two sets of contending factions. The people themselves—the deprived—hide in their shacks whenever the terrorists of the right (the army) come to "protect" them or the terrorists of the left (the guerrillas) come to "liberate" them.

Meanwhile, the United States supplies arms to the governments in power while other countries supply arms to the rebel forces, and both factions use those weapons to shoot bystanders. "Rightists"—"leftists"—the terms don't make much difference. Both sides are obsessed with the old notion that power comes from the barrel of a gun.

American sponsorship of authoritarian regimes has aided in the spread of terrorism not only in Latin America but in other parts of the world. The governments of Thailand, Indonesia, the Philippines, Zaire—all in the U.S. sphere of influence—have used terror to maintain power and to protect the profits and privileges of the elite. Abroad, official agencies of the U.S. government have attempted assassination of foreign leaders. The CIA's record, according to John Stockwell, one of that agency's former officers,

> includes the assassinations of Patrice Lumumba [prime minister of Congo]; Ngo Dinh Diem, the South Vietnamese President; Rafael Trujillo Molina, the Dominican Republic President; Gen. Rene Schneider, the commander-in-chief of the Chilean army; plus several bloody covert wars, and a deadly terrorist program in Vietnam called Phoenix that the CIA says involved the killing of 22,000 Vietnamese.

Former CIA agents have made a profitable business out of training terrorists for hostile foreign governments. In 1980 Edwin P. Wilson and Frank E. Terpil were indicted by a Federal grand jury on charges of illegally shipping explosives to Libya as part of that country's terrorist training operations. (Wilson was found guilty after trial in 1983.) They also recruited former Green Berets, men trained by the U.S. Army to be America's elite commando troops, to staff the terrorist training program in Libya. One of the ex-Green Berets, Luke Thompson, who signed on for Libya, told *The*

New York Times that he took part in plotting an attempt to assassinate a guerrilla leader in the Dominican Republic in 1965.

Thompson claims, said the *Times*, that

> his colleagues later went to Bolivia where they helped government soldiers hunt down and assassinate Ernesto Ché Guevara, the Cuban revolutionary leader. In Southeast Asia, Thompson says he and his fellow Green Berets assassinated province chiefs, businessmen and political leaders suspected of being Vietcong sympathizers, made reconaissance missions into North Vietnam and carried out secret attacks in Cambodia months before the formal American incursion in 1970.

When Thompson and other former Green Berets flew to Libya, they were taken to an explosives laboratory in Tripoli. They found a group of American ordnance experts there, mostly military veterans, instructing Libyans how to manufacture terrorist bombs.

How does it happen, asks *Times* reporter Philip Taubman, that a group of former Green Berets, "who consider themselves unwavering American patriots," are willing to make money by helping another country's terrorist operations? Perhaps because they got so used to this kind of job, they thought nothing wrong with it. As Taubman put it, Thompson was, after all, "part of a secret American army of covert agents who handled the dirty work of United States foreign policy—often under the supervision of the C.I.A.—all over the world."

Chapter 15

The Goal of Life

What about the morality of terrorism?

Is there ever justification for terrorist tactics?

Can a case be made out in defense of Sophia Perovskaya's assassination of the tsar? Of Alexander Berkman's attempt on the life of Frick? Of the Stern Gang or the PLO? Of the Tupamaros, the Red Brigades, Baader-Meinhof, the Weather Underground?

Terrorist incidents have always provoked intense criticism. Sometimes the disapproval comes from people or governments with biases that make them suspect. If the government of South Africa—which uses indiscriminate violence against its own people—protests terrorism, we know the real reason is that it opposes social change in general, whether violent or nonviolent.

But many critics of terrorism themselves want and work for social change. Some of these believe that certain limited forms of violence can be justified. It is indiscriminate terrorism that they hold to be morally wrong. Assassinating a Hitler or a Stalin can be morally justified, they think. The killer of such a leader fights a limited war and discriminates in his choice of targets. Both Hitler and Stalin were dictators whose taste for mass murder went far beyond the use of enough power to keep them in office. But not even tyrannicide in such cases would be justified, it is argued, unless there would be an appreciable difference between the tyrant and his likely successor. If it is merely another dictator of the same bloody kind who takes power, then the assassination is much less justifiable.

It is the sort of terrorism that makes no distinction between the guilty and the innocent that most hold to be morally unjustifiable. And there have been numbers of terrorists who agreed with this view. Sophia Perovskaya and her group were among them.

We've seen, however, that in our time many of the terrorist groups do kill indiscriminately. They blow up airplanes, bomb restaurants, wreck trains. Aren't their victims innocent? No, the terrorists answer, everyone shares in the responsibility for society's injustice. Recall that after Emile Henry bombed a crowded Paris café he told the court, "There are no innocent people." And the kidnapped Sir Geoffrey Jackson said that his Tupamaro captors told him, "There is no such thing as an innocent bystander."

Terrorists fighting for national liberation call their movements a form of war, and war almost always brings injury or death to civilians. One official of al-Fatah, the PLO group commanded by Yasir Arafat, once said, "The deaths are regrettable, but they are a fact of war in which innocents become involved."

Another argument the terrorists offer is that the oppressed people they claim to act for have suffered harm. And if what the terrorists do causes other people to die, that's what happens unavoidably when you try to right a serious wrong.

Sometimes it's the government that is blamed for the indiscriminate violence of a terrorist group. Yes, the terrorists admit, we killed innocent people, but it was only because the government would not allow peaceful change. That left violence as the only means of bringing about change. In Argentina a terrorist group said they had lost faith in elections as the way to accomplish change. "Power," they stated, "is not born from votes. Power is born from gunpoint." This last is now like a slogan emblazoned on terrorist banners.

Another justification holds that the government practices indiscriminate violence, so what else is the opposition to do but react to that violence with terrorism?

What hasn't been looked into yet is the central question: Does the end justify the means? Early in their lives Emma Goldman and Alexander Berkman believed the answer was yes. That thinking led them to tinker with a time bomb in a crowded tenement, putting the lives of innocent people in danger. It led them to believe that by taking one man's life, they would help the working class gain freedom. As Goldman's biographer, Richard Drinnon, put it: "The fullness of life was to be achieved by destroying life."

Goldman soon outgrew her belief in the end justifying the means. While her study of history convinced her that great changes will always be violent, she could still say, "I feel violence in whatever form never has and probably never will bring constructive results."

That dilemma of means and ends torments revolutionaries. Terrorists often settle the issue for themselves by deciding that private scruples must be forgotten when the good of the cause is at stake. They see themselves as the instruments of justice. They kill, there is blood on their hands, but it is honored by the rightness of their cause. They lie, they cheat, they steal, they murder, but they see these sins as trivial measured by the great end in view. Such immoral means are sacrifices they must make upon the altar of necessity.

The ideal goals of justice and equality and freedom become political rationalizations for the acts of terror. Such left-wing terrorists place the interests of humankind in the *future* above the interests of people in the *present*. A glorious end justifies the most inglorious means.

Most people try to live by a code of ethics that respects the individual, treats him as an end in himself, and seeks to love him. The code of the terrorist treats the individual as a cog in the machine, as raw material to be manipulated for society's good. *They*—the terrorists and their revolutionary party—decide what that good is and the path that must be taken to achieve it.

The radical goal they have in mind is the end that justifies the use of any means.

In reality, ends and means cannot be separated. The revolutionary whose goal is some kind of dictatorship leaves no room for individual dissent. His party, and his party alone, *knows* what the new society must be; it will decide everything for the good of all in the one-party state of the future. And in the struggle to make that revolution, the same kind of thinking operates. The revolutionary will decide what means to use, and woe to those who differ.

A long time ago, in the nineteenth century, the Russian radical Alexander Herzen warned against sanctifying crimes by faith in some remote utopia. The cut-and-dried schemes of such "liberators," he said, are bound to straitjacket humanity. Any methods that assume there are simple, radical solutions always lead in the end to oppression and bloodshed. Formulas are what such radicals live by, not actual experience. Who can guarantee that any such formula will bring about happiness or a more rational life?

Like other humane thinkers, Herzen believed any attempt to dedicate people to the service of an abstraction always leads in the end to making them victims. And no matter how noble the abstraction is—justice, progress, liberty. The way people live and their relationships with others make them far too complex for neat solutions. If you try to force them into an abstract formula, it ends with doing injury to them. Maybe some—the leaders?—are liberated, but only at the cost of enslaving others. An old tyranny is replaced by a new and sometimes far worse one.

Look at the crimes committed by terrorists as reported so frequently in your daily newspaper. In the name of some unpredictable future, of something that may never happen, the terrorists assert these acts of violence are sanctified. Would anyone deny that these same acts of violence would be monstrous if they were done for some selfish purpose?

No, each generation is unique and precious. The life of each one of us is unique and precious, too. The purpose of the struggle for liberty is not liberty tomorrow, it is liberty today. Sacrificing the present to some vague and unpredictable future is a delusion. The notion that humanity has a splendid future, guaranteed by history, can justify the most appalling cruelties in the present.

The goal of life is life itself.

Bibliography

Titles marked with asterisks (*) are paperback editions. Those with daggers (†) are hardcover books also available in paperback.

Alpert, Jane. *Growing Up Underground: A Remarkable Autobiography Which Becomes the Reflection of an Era.* New York: William Morrow and Company, Inc., 1981.

*Arendt, Hannah. *Crises of the Republic.* New York: Harcourt Brace Jovanovich, Inc., 1972.

†Avrich, Paul. *The Russian Anarchists.* New York: W. W. Norton & Company, Inc., 1978.

Becker, Jillian. *Hitler's Children: The Story of the Baader-Meinhof Terrorist Gang.* New York: J. B. Lippincott Company, 1977.

†Bell, J. Bowyer. *Terror out of Zion: The Irgun, Lehi, Stern and the Palestine Underground, 1929–1949.* New York: St. Martin's Press, Inc., 1977.

†Berlin, Isaiah. *Russian Thinkers.* New York: The Viking Press, Inc., 1978.

*Bickel, Alexander M. *The Morality of Consent.* New Haven, Ct.: Yale University Press, 1975.

Broido, Vera. *Apostles into Terrorists.* New York: The Viking Press, Inc., 1977.

Clarke, Thurston. *By Blood and Fire: The Attack on the King David Hotel.* New York: G. P. Putnam's Sons, 1981.

Dellinger, David. *More Power Than We Know: The People's Movement toward Democracy.* Garden City, N.Y.: Anchor Books, Doubleday & Company, Inc., 1975.

*Diggins, John P. *The American Left in the Twentieth Century.* New York: Harcourt Brace Jovanovich, Inc., 1973.

Dobson, Christopher, and Ronald Payne. *Counterattack: The West's Battle against the Terrorists.* New York: Facts On File, 1982.

*Drinnon, Richard. *Rebel in Paradise: A Biography of Emma Goldman.* Chicago: University of Chicago Press, 1961.

Evans, Ernest. *Calling a Truce to Terror: The American Response to International Terrorism.* Westport, Ct.: Greenwood Press, 1979.

*Frank, Gerold. *The Deed.* New York: Berkley Publishing Corp., 1979.

*Goldman, Emma. *Living My Life.* New York: Meridian Books, New American Library, Inc., 1977.

*Harrington, Michael. *Fragments of the Century.* New York: Simon & Schuster, Inc., 1977.

Herman, Edward S. *The Real Terror Network.* Boston: South End Press, 1982.

*Hofstadter, Richard, and Michael Wallace, eds. *American Violence: A Documentary History.* New York: Random House, Inc., 1971.

*Holland, Jack. *Too Long a Sacrifice: Life and Death in*

Northern Ireland since 1969. Baltimore: Penguin Books, Inc., 1982.

*Howe, Irving. *Beyond the New Left*. New York: Horizon Press Publications, 1972.

———. "The Return of Terror." *Dissent*, Summer 1975, pp. 227–37.

Hyams, Edward. *Terrorists and Terrorism*. New York: St. Martin's Press, Inc., 1974.

*Joll, James. *The Anarchists*. Boston: Harvard University Press, 1980.

*Kraditor, Aileen S. *The Radical Persuasion, 1890–1917*. Baton Rouge, La.: Louisiana State University Press, 1981.

*Laqueur, Walter. *Terrorism*. Boston: Little, Brown and Company, 1979.

*———, ed. *The Terrorism Reader*. New York: New American Library, Inc., 1978.

MacKinley, James. *Assassination in America*. New York: Harper & Row, Publishers, 1977.

Malia, Martin. *Alexander Herzen and the Birth of Russian Socialism*. Washington, D.C.: Howard University Press, 1961.

Mehnert, Klaus. *Twilight of the Young: The Radical Movements of the 1960s and Their Legacy*. New York: Holt, Rinehart and Winston, Inc., 1978.

Meltzer, Milton. *The Human Rights Book*. New York: Farrar, Straus & Giroux, Inc., 1979.

O'Brien, Conor Cruise. "Reflections on Terrorism." *New York Review of Books*, September 16, 1976, pp. 44–48.

Oglesby, Carl, ed. *The New Left Reader*. New York: Grove Press, Inc., 1969.

*O'Neill, William L. *Coming Apart: An Informal History of America in the 1960s*. New York: Times Books, 1971.

Parry, Albert. *Terrorism: From Robespierre to Arafat*. New York: Vanguard Press, Inc., 1976.

Payne, Robert. *The Terrorists*. New York: Funk & Wagnalls, Inc., 1957.

Smith, Colin. *Carlos: Portrait of a Terrorist*. New York: Holt, Rinehart and Winston, Inc., 1976.

†Sterling, Claire. *The Terror Network*. New York: Holt, Rinehart and Winston, Inc., 1981.

Van Voris, William H. *Violence in Ulster: An Oral Documentary*. Amherst, Mass.: University of Massachusetts Press, 1975.

*Walzer, Michael. *Just and Unjust Wars*. New York: Basic Books, Inc., Publishers, 1977.

*Wilkinson, Paul. *Political Terrorism*. New York: Halsted Press, John Wiley & Sons, Inc., 1976.

*———. *Terrorism and the Liberal State*. New York: New York University Press, 1979.

*Woodcock, George. *Anarchism: A History of Libertarian Ideas and Movements*. New York: New American Library, 1962.

INDEX

Numbers in *italics* refer to illustrations.